Download New York State of Mind 1.0 FREE!

There are hundreds of interviews and dozens of **Behind The Music Tales** series books to follow.

That's why I am giving you a copy **of New York State of Mind 1.0** for FREE!

Get exclusive 1992 and 1993 interviews with Tragedy Khadafi, Brand Nubian, and Pete Rock & C.L. Smooth FREE!

I am only looking for your email. You will receive emails with updates on new releases, exclusive images, original audio, and be eligible for free advance copies of series books. **You can opt out at any time.**

http://eepurl.com/ckHZdb

Behind The Music Tales Books

N.W.A: The Aftermath

The Real Eminem: Broke City Trash Rapper

The Real Destiny's Child: The Writing's On The Wall

New York State of Mind 1.0

The Reasonings of Buju Banton, Bounty Killer & Sizzla

Magnolia: Home of tha Soldiers (Behind the Scenes with the Cash Money Millionaires)

The Real 213

The Real MC Eiht: Geah!

The Real Diddy

The Real Daft Punk

Praise for Harris Rosen

This guy! I plead the fifth. This guy is nuts."
- Eminem

"Dope questions, man. Very insightful, very thoughtful."
- Guru (Gang Starr)

"You like a Psychiatrist or some shit? This shit is just coming out but go ahead."
- Mary J. Blige

"Definitely a real interview! Digging deep up in there, man. Not afraid to ask questions!"
- K-Ci Hailey (Jodeci)

"The Wizard asked me for a copy of your magazine."
- Guy-Manuel de Homem-Christo (Daft Punk)

"You didn't wear your glasses, and you haven't carried your hearing aid. What else is wrong with you?"
- Bushwick Bill

"Peace and blessing, Brother Harris. Thank you for inspiring my words. Keep 'yo balance."
- Erykah Badu

"Can I see that pen?"
- Bobby Brown

"What else do you want to know? Talk to me."
- Aaliyah

Copyright

© 2016 by Peace! Carving and Harris Rosen.

All rights reserved under International and Pan American Copyright Conventions. The Author has provided this ebook for your personal use only. It may not be resold or transferred to others. You may not make this ebook publicly available in any way. No part of this ebook may be reproduced or transmitted in any form by any means, electronic, mechanical, scanned, recording, or distributed in any printed, or audio form without written permission.

Published by Peace! Carving

First edition

First published in November 2016

ISBN: 978-0-9953072-4-7 (Print)

ISBN: 978-0-9953072-3-0 (Digital)

Mr. Heller Press

Heller HQ

QB

Spadina-Fort York

Toronto, ON m5v 2b3

Canada

Dedication

This series is dedicated to my son Louis, late father, mother, sister, grandmother & the late Raymond Wallace.

Thank you for a lifetime of support and encouragement. I would not be here without you.

Acknowledgments

I wish to thank the following people for their contributions to my inspiration and knowledge and other help in creating this book:
Mark Reed, Rob Harris, Peter Cherniawski, Josh Roter, Arty, Shahroze Ilyas, Ian Steaman, Eon Sinclair, Jr., Todd DeKoker, Phil Demetro, Peter Lazanik, Rishi Persaud.

Contents

Preface 1

Chapter 1: We Be The Cash Money Millionaires 5

Chapter 2: I'm An Untamed Guerilla 9

Turk Album Discography 18

Chapter 3: Shit I Kick Be Real 19

B.G. Album Discography 30

Chapter 4: I Don't Get Caught In The Mist 31

Juvenile Album Discography 45

Chapter 5: I'm Gonna Live And Die In This Here 47

Lil Wayne Album Discography 66

Official Lil Wayne Mixtapes 68

Chapter 6: This Year I Got A Space Shuttle Parked Out Around The Corner 71

Mannie Fresh Album Discography 80

Chapter 7: I Look At It We Got To Hustlin' 81

Birdman Album Discography 86

Chapter 8: I Ain't Gonna Let Nobody Else Guide Our Destiny 87

Who Is Harris Rosen? 111
Other Books By Harris Rosen 112

Preface

Cash Money Records set the music industry on fire in 1998 when they signed an unprecedented $30 000 000 pressing and distribution contract with Universal Music Group that encompassed a $3 000 000 advance, 85% of royalties, 50% publishing and full ownership of master recordings.

Cash Money Records began as an independent movement out of New Orleans. Louisiana, in 1991, started by visionary street hustlers and brothers, Ronald and Bryan Williams. Known for its subtropical temperate climate, New Orleans 90°F summer weathers and high humidity cast an ominous shade. Sensing the Hip-Hop industry was set to expand and spread beyond the strongholds of New York and California to the South and further, the Williams brothers invested their monies and began to sign local New Orleans based and regional artists to the label.

Step-by-step they carved out an impressive niche while building on the core of Bounce music. Albums came from the likes of Kilo G, Lil' Slim, U.N.L.V., Pimp Daddy, Ms. Tee, and Mr. Ivan, and hungry new artists were recruited to join them in the movement. B.G. recorded his first album, **Real Story**, for Cash Money Records in 1994, as the 14 year old head of a group called B.G.'z with a 12 years old Lil Wayne. At the time, B.G. went by Lil Doogie and Lil Wayne was known as Baby D.

Then, in 1996, they held steadfast to the principles and the knowledge that put them over and cleaned house dropping every artist from the label except one, whom they had personally groomed for stardom, and placed their bets. Unfortunately, Lil Wayne was on an extended hiatus from his career due to family issues, and B.G. was the last man standing.

B.G. released his solo debut, **Chopper City,** in February 1996, and it moved from there. The Williams brothers connected with New Orleans Bounce sensation Juvenile, who had recently become a free agent, and he joined the ranks. Lil Wayne returned to the game. Slim and Baby's cousin, Bulletproof a.k.a. Lil Derrick, was in the mix but he was too devoted to the streets. A young and hungry Turk was drafted up and the Hot Boys were born.

Each member still a teenager.

Concurrent with the growth of the label and its artists, local DJ star and producer Mannie Fresh, who joined Cash Money Records in the early stages to head their production, was crafting a sound of his own based on a mix of Miami Bass, Bounce, Hip-Hop and a heady assortment of musical influences. Responsible for producing and engineering every song for the label. He took New Orleans trademark call and response Bounce party music to the next level.

Heads began to turn, and the music industry took notice in 1997 when what once was a small independent label started selling hundreds of thousands of albums with releases by B.G., Juvenile and the Hot Boys landing on the Billboard charts every other month. Many labels came calling, but none offered the right deal until Universal Music Group.

Everything came together with the release of Juvenile's **400 Degreez** albums on November 3, 1998. Armed with the national distribution and promotion of Universal, and the production wizardry of Mannie Fresh, the album went on to sell over 4 million copies on the strength of his breakthrough single "Ha" and its massive follow-up "Back That Azz Up". Compatriot B.G. followed with his landmark trendsetting single "Bling Bling" of **Chopper City in the Ghetto** in the spring of 1999. Fifteen-year-old Lil Wayne joined in on the success when his debut full-length offering, Tha Block Is Hot hit in the winter of 1999. Cash Money Records mania and New Orleans slang became omnipresent.

The in-person interviews featured here with Turk, Juvenile, Lil Wayne, B.G., Mannie Fresh, Ronald "Godfather Slim" Williams and Bryan "Baby" Williams, occurred in mid-November 1999 on the set of Cash Money Records debut film offering, **Baller Blockin'.** Set deep in the heart of the notorious 3rd Ward Magnolia Projects of New Orleans, LA, the film speaks to Project life and the corruption of the Police force.

The set was brimming with activity. The community came out in force to see what was going down and be seen, and a few managed to hustle up a sandwich of their own from catering. Godfather Slim was my designated point person, and he ensured the "Boys" made themselves available when not filming a scene.

With that said, what was designated as a one day trip became two as the film, and next business took precedence.

Lil Wayne was set to celebrate the first birthday of his daughter, Reginae.

B.G. was rumoured to have recently overcome a heroin habit. Juvenile was primed and ready to release **Tha G-Code**. Young Turk hung tough in the cut waiting for his opportunity to follow suit with a full-length of his own.

A spirited game of dice on the tour bus between B.G., Lil Wayne and a few of the immediate Cash Money Records family saw money won and lost. Mannie Fresh and Baby, who also partnered up as the Big Tymers, stood to politick with a small crew sipping on a case of Louis Roederer Cristal out of red solo cups. I will never forget Mannie Fresh saying that while others sought out and collected advance music. He had a taste for advance cars.

The interviews run in the order they occurred. Baby, consumed with business and who knows what else was brief and to the point, but he did manage to pop in and join Mannie Fresh and speak of the Big Tymers experience.

This is the Cash Money Millionaires: Ronald "Godfather Slim" Williams, Bryan "Baby" Williams, Mannie Fresh, B.G., Juvenile, Young Turk, and Lil Wayne. Direct from the Magnolia Projects, home of tha soldiers, way back in November 1999.

Disclaimer

Opinions expressed in the interviews are not necessarily those of the Author.

CHAPTER 1

WE BE THE CASH MONEY MILLIONAIRES

Cash Money Records was in full bloom in the summer of 1999. From the fall of 1998, through the summer of 1999, the label had sold millions of albums. Juvenile's **400 Degreez** led the charge on the strength of monster singles "Ha" and "Back That Azz Up"; B.G. dominated the spring with certified classic "Bling Bling"; and Hot Boys heated up the summer with "I Need A Hot Girl". Back to back to back to back hits, that placed them on the tip of everyone's tongue.

The fact is the label, and its artists remained a mystery to most beyond their stronghold in the South. Yes, people around the world now knew their music and movement but they had not conducted a national tour or crossed over into the mainstream media eye.

The eyes of the world on them, CEO Ronald "Godfather Slim" Williams took Juvenile and Turk on a road trip the final week of August 1999, to the MAGIC trade show, the world's largest fashion marketplace, in Las Vegas, Nevada. A legion of artists, young entrepreneurs and savvy businesspersons filled its urban aisles with swagger and bravado like no other every February and August. Composed of bustling lifestyle communities, it had given birth to the billion-dollar urban fashion industry making attendance mandatory, if you were in any way associated with the game, shared aspirations to join, or hustled for a living.

Blinging through the aisles, the Cash Money Records crew ensured their presence felt, and Juvenile and Turk performed a small club show to double-up and made sure. In the midst of one of many aisles stopping jaunts, Juvenile and Godfather Slim provided a brief update and peak at what lay ahead.

***

What is Cash Money?

Juvenile:
We be the Cash Money Millionaires. We all a clique. It ain't just about Juvenile. It's all from the CEO's, the brother's Bryan and Ronald Williams, Turk, the Hot Boys. We all a camp. It just so happen that my album came out first, but it ain't even like that. We all a camp. We all ride together, we all runnin' together. You ain't gonna see me - If you see me all these people gonna be with me everywhere we go.

How long have you been doing this? Cash Money Records has many albums.

Godfather Slim:
We been doing this eight years, man. We put out like thirty albums. Eight years.

How come it took so long to blow?

Godfather Slim:
We was waiting on something that satisfies the company, the artists, to make everybody happy. A lot of people get twisted in this game and gonna take whatever. So we all comfortable, we all happy. My people happy so I'm straight.

What's coming up?

Godfather Slim:
B.G.'s new album is coming up. The Hot Boys, who Juvenile is one of the members; you got Wayne, Turk and B.G. Big Tymers new album. Juvenile second album G-Code about to come out Lil Wayne solo. So we got a lot of stuff. Turk solo.

Juvenile:
We got some shit up our sleeve, man. Like I said, I'll say it today; I'll say it next year around the same time. After '99 over we gonna run this motherfucker. A nigga gonna have to kiss ass and all that to get with us. That's how the game go.

CHAPTER 2

I'M AN UNTAMED GUERILLA

Young Turk was born Tab Virgil, Jr., February 8, 1981.

Turk states he came up the same as the "average Black man" hustling to put food on the table to "get it as they live." He was put in place to the Cash Money Records crew at a neighbourhood block party by female artist Magnolia Shorty. He called and bothered the Williams brothers until he was asked to come to the studio where he contributed to three songs on Juvenile's **Solja Rags** album: "I Did That", "Hide Out or Ride Out", and "Spittin Game". He then featured on the debut Hot Boys album. **Get It How U Live!!**, which arrived here on October 28, 1997.

At the time of this feature interview, Turk had experienced multi-platinum success as a member of the Hot Boys and on album appearances with his Cash Money Records brothers. His solo album debut lay 18 months ahead.

What's your role with Cash Money?

Turk:

We don't have no role around here, do what you're doing and do it well, that's all.

When is your solo album dropping?

Turk:

Next year, 2000. I don't know what day or month but next year 2000 it be hitting the streets.

Did you grow up in this area of the Magnolia?

Turk:

I'm in Kenner right now. I grew up around Robinson Street in front of the school in the Magnolia Project.

What did you do coming up?

Turk:

What an average Black man do; hustle. You got to put food on the table. Get it how they live.

How vital is hustlin' to the whole Project?

Turk:

My momma at the time she was strugglin'. My daddy, he was an old wino. He ain't do nothing for me, and I didn't want to see us … We had two - There was three of us. It was hard for my mom, and by me being the oldest I felt like I had to what I had to do, so I started hustlin'.

Is that how you ran into everyone else in the crew?

Turk:

No. One day they came around here at a DJ. Call it a DJ; everybody gets together. Niggas would be playing outside, and they popped up, and Magnolia Shorty, a female artist they had a year, two years ago, she introduced me to 'em, and I went up to 'em, they gave me a card. I kept calling them, bothering them, told me to come to the studio. I got on one of Juvenile's albums he was doing his album. I got on about three songs and the rest history, the new Cash Money.

How did you end up in Hot Boys?

Turk:
They put all us together. All of us came as solo artists, and they had this dude around here named Gangster. He thought of the idea. He was like, 'Hot Boys, Hot Boys.' He explained what a Hot Boy was and we like we got that. We drive fly. We got gold in our mouth. We got hoes, ya dig. So we the Hot Boys, and the rest history on that.

What would you say a Hot Boy is?

Turk:
I just told 'ya. A paper chaser who got they block on fire, remaining a G until the moment they expire. That's a Hot Boy.

How do you keep your mind on the music when all this is going on around you?

Turk:
You got to stay focused. This is something I love. It's something you love you gonna keep it in your heart, get it right and keep it right.

What's with No Limit and their Hot Boys?

Turk:
I don't want to talk about No Limit. This Cash Money, man.

When you work in the studio with Mannie Fresh does he come with beats and then you come in and rhyme over them? How does that work?

Turk:
We all be in there together as a whole family. He do the beat; we do the rhyme right there. We do an album in like two weeks.

What concepts are you coming with for your album?

Turk:
Everyday life street shit, Project shit. We sling it how we talk it, talk it like we walk it.

Are you still living the life?

Turk:
No, I ain't living the life, but if I had to, I know how to do it. I ain't no hoe. See, some people get wrapped the fuck up. I'm still a guerrilla. Can you still walk around this area and get love?

Turk:
Yes, indeed. I be back here every day. This is all I know. I ain't no suburb nigga. I'm a Project nigga, man. It's all I know. That's why we understand what the people want. That's why we selling so many records.

How many records are you selling now?

Turk:
Millions and millions. I know you look at the Billboard. You see them triangles.

Would you say that you're all young entrepreneurs?

Turk:
Yeah, mmmm hmmm, yep. All of us. None of us over 20. We all young, from 15 to 20.

Who is 15?

Turk:
Lil Wayne. I'm 16.

Lil Wayne is 15 years old selling millions of records.

Turk:
Yep.

Are you giving back to the community?

Turk:
We're giving back to the community. Come and shoot movies. We ain't forget where we come from. Every now and then we'll buy the kids stuff, do things for kids, show our face.

Magnolia: Home of tha Soldiers

How did you get into this?

Turk:
I saw Juvenile. I saw all of them rapping. I used to play sports. I was like damn, this is easy money right there. At first, I was in it for the fame and fortune; then I start loving it. Here I am Lil Turk, Young Turk.

What else do you want people to know?

Turk:
Look out for Untamed Guerrilla. Hold on; I'm eating a ham sandwich right now. Look out for Untamed Guerrilla in 2000, Lil Turk album.

Why are you calling it that?

Turk:
"'Cause I'm an untamed guerrilla. I'm untamed and wild.

How wild do you get?

Turk:
Let a nigga fuck with me, they'll see.

Turk's debut solo album **Young & Thuggin** was released on June 5, 2001, and immediately entered the Billboard Top 10 selling 82 000 copies its first week. He parted ways with the Hot Boys and eventually left Cash Money Records to pursue a solo career on his own in 2003, signing a deal with respected New Orleans producer Ke'Noe's Laboratory Recordz. He recorded two albums for the label, **Raw & Uncut** in 2003 and **Penitentiary Chances** in 2004, before getting caught up in street life and jailed.

Turk was convicted and sentenced in Memphis, Tennessee, to 10 years and a fine of $200 000 on August 24, 2005, for being a felon, drug addict, and in possession of a firearm. A S.W.A.T. team raid had entered the apartment he was in searching for drugs and weapons and were greeted by 9 mm gunfire. One Deputy was shot in the jaw, hip and leg and another in the neck. On April 26, 2006, Turk pleaded not guilty for attempted first-degree murder and was sentenced to an agreed-upon 12 years incarceration for the same case, to avoid a 25-year sentence. During his jail term, Laboratory Recordz released two albums, **Still A Hot Boy** in 2005, and **Convicted Felons** in 2006.

Turk was released from prison on October 12, 2012, after serving almost nine years. On December 1, 2012, He marked his return to the music industry with "Zip It" featuring Lil Wayne. Juvenile joined in on the remix released December 27, 2012, and then B.G. completed the Hot Boy reunion when the song appeared on the Turk mixtape **Blame It On The System**, hosted by DJ Holiday, released February 23, 2013.

Turk signed a contract with Rap-A-Lot Records in December 2013, for his own label Young & Thuggin' to be distributed by Sony Red, and stopped any Hot Boys reunion. He released the **Get Money Stay Real** mixtape hosted by DJ Hektik on October 30, 2014.

In February 2015, Turk sued Cash Money Records for rights to his music void. In May 2015, a Louisiana District Court Judge granted Turk a default motion with the damages to be assessed. Turk's legal team then issued subpoenas to Universal Music Group and Universal Music Publishing Group to access the accounting records for Cash Money Records. An undisclosed out of court settlement was paid by Cash Money Records, and the case dismissed on June 30, 2015, at Turk's request.

Turk has experienced a renaissance of sorts in 2016 with multiple hot new songs and videos releases as a solo, featured, and guest artist, including new music with the Hot Boys. He posted to Instagram in the early a.m. of July 3, 2016, stating he is now back with Cash Money Records and never left; "Yea I Signed Back With #CashMoneyRecords." Later he posted to Twitter "I Never Left #CashMoneyRecords I Just Went To Prison And Got My Mind And Heart Right!!! #YNT #CashMoneyRichGang."

Turk is currently working on new music, an autobiography, ***The AutoThugography of Turk***, and a screenplay about his life, ***Reckless***.

TURK ALBUM DISCOGRAPHY

- **Young & Thuggin'** - June 5, 2001 (Cash Money Records)
- **Raw & Uncut** - October 21, 2003 (Laboratory Recordz)
- **Penitentiary Chances** - April 27, 2004 (Laboratory Recordz)
- **Still A Hot Boy** - September 13, 2005 (Laboratory Recordz)
- **Convicted Felons** - September 5, 2006 (Laboratory Recordz)

Hot Boys

- **Get It How U Live!!** - October 28, 1997 (Cash Money Records)
- **Guerilla Warfare** - July 27, 1999 (Cash Money Records)
- **Let 'Em Burn** - March 25, 2003 (Cash Money Records)

B.G. was born Christopher Dorsey, September 3, 1980.

B.G. was the first Hot Boy signed to Cash Money Records. His Father was killed when he was young. Cash Money Records owners Ronald and Bryan Williams stepped in as "big brothers" and played a major role in his life helping his Mother raise him. Dubbed Lil Doogie, He was paired up with Lil Wayne, then known as Baby D, and together the duo recorded their first album **True Story** for Cash Money Records as the BG'z. Two songs, the title track "True Story" and "Fuck Big Boy" directed at fellow New Orleans Rapper, Mystikal and his label Big Boy Records. It was initially released on July 28, 1995, and then reissued as a straight B.G. album by the label on June 29, 1999.

B.G. stayed in the studio recording for the next four years and released four solo underground classics: ***Chopper City, It's All On U Vol. 1, It's All On U Vol. 2*** and ***Chopper City In The Ghetto***. All of them with Mannie Fresh behind the boards. His Cash Money Records partners, Big Tymers, Lil Wayne, Juvenile, Turk and special guests contributed to each release, and in tune, B.G. enriched their solo releases too.

A real street hustler to the core, the profound concepts and silver-tongued baritone of B.G. crossed over far and wide reaching and affecting Projects and low-income people all over the world. He has sold millions of albums and enraptured the Rap universe while simultaneously tuning them in and turning them on to the "Bling Bling" lifestyle of the rich and infamous Cash Money Millionaires.

***

Who is B.G.?

B.G.:
B.G., that's me. One of the original Hot Boys. B.G. a laid back nigga who be chilling, handling his business, dropping gangsta shit, that's all.

Counting money?

B.G.:
Yeah, about to go get off in a dice game.

Is there a B.G. state of mind?

B.G.:
Nah, not really. I be in all kind of zones. I be in a rapping zone; I be in a fucking a ho zone; I be chilling, man. I'm me all the way around the clock, same 'ol nigga all the time.

What do you want to put across? Do you have a message?

B.G.:
I mean, keep it real with yourself. Keep it real with niggas you been fucking with. Don't let nobody fuck over you. Handle your business, man. Man, I want niggas to feel me, man. Let 'em know Cash Money the shit, Cash Money got talent, and Cash Money got this industry by the nuts. I want niggas to respect my mind, that's all.

You're the transitional artists for Cash Money. You're the first Rapper to throw it down Cash Money style.

B.G.:
Mmm hmmm.

What was it like back then and why were you the first?

B.G.:
I've been doing this since I was like ten years old. The label started in like '92, and they signed me in '92, and I've just been doing it ever since. Holding it down, man. Me and 'Lil Wayne, yep. At first, it was me and 'Lil Wayne. We had a group called the BG'z. Then he had some family problems; he had to drift away, so I went solo as the B.G. Then he came back, then Juve came, and Turk came. We formed a group, The Hot Boys. We just been doing our thing.

Where do the brothers come in?

B.G.:
Who that? Bryan and Ronald? They is Cash Money Records. They the owners of the label, they started it. They come in - They play a major role in my life. They helped my mama raise me when my daddy got killed, so they like my big brothers. It's all good.

What's life like as B.G.?

B.G.:
It's all good. I ain't really want for nothing. I ain't hurtin'. I got money, I got hoes. my family's straight, travelin,' ya dig. Platinum albums, see what I'm sayin'? It's just all good.

How do you keep your mind on the music when all that shit is going around you?

B.G.:
That's my life. That's all I know. That's all I got. I dropped out of school in tenth grade, so I can't get no job. They don't hire you without no High School diploma, but I'm in the process of getting my G.E.D. now. Rap, that's all I got, that's my life. I write everyday. I stay 'cause I know what's gonna give me pay, and Rap is gonna take me to the bank.

Why are your lyrics so deep? What's going on in your mind?

B.G.:
I've been through it all. I've been through it all a juvenile to go through. From hustlin,' to jackin,' stealing cars, jail, whatever. I'm in the ghetto. I'm in the streets day for day. Even though I got money that still don't change me. I see what's going on around me, so I give niggas what they can feel, and all hoods the same. All ghettos the same all across the world. That's why niggas respect my mind and know it ain't no fantasise. Shit, I kick be real.

What role does pushing weight play?

B.G.:
It don't play no role in my life 'cause I done gave it up. That ain't me no more. I slang raps.

But that helped sculpt you as a person, sculpt your head.

B.G.:
Yeah, yeah, yeah, without a doubt. I learned from the best.

Would you say a record company is a good move for young entrepreneurs to invest their money?

B.G.:
If they know what they doing if they real with it. If it's in they heart and they gonna go the whole nine with it, yes.

So the brothers came up in the game like you, and they just manifested and put their loot into the label?

B.G.:
Yeah, I guess you could say that.

Why does New Orleans have so many drugs and poverty?

B.G.:
I can't say. It's like that all over. We ain't the only city with drugs. We don't grow it here. It comes from Cuba, somewhere. I don't know where it comes from, but when it gets there, niggas do what they got to do to get paid.

Why were you the guy they came to take the label to the next level?

B.G.:
Me and Mannie Fresh we just got this collaboration. That's the only nigga who ever done beats with me throughout my time being in the industry. He feels me, and I feel him. They believed in me and I believin' in them. They kept it real with me, and I kept it real with them. We stick together like a family, man. I felt as though everything was riding on me at one time 'cause I was like the only artist left on the label. We wasn't about to give up and throw our hands in, so we got in the studio, got down and dirty, and we kept it going, and like I said. Lil Wayne came, Juve came, Turk came. Here we go today, but it's all good.

Is there a go-to guy in the organisation, or is everybody equal?

B.G.:
Everybody equal. We all family. We all family.

A magazine said you had a drug addiction.

B.G.:
I care not to talk about that ... That's it?

A couple of your albums are Chopper City.

B.G.:
Just two of 'em. One of 'em is **Chopper City**, and one of 'em is **Chopper City in the Ghetto**. My second album was called Chopper City. Chopper, that's another word for AK47. That's all they carry down here, so I call it Chopper City. **Chopper City in the Ghetto**, that's like my fifth solo album, so I went back and listened to my second album, and I was like I'm gonna go **Chopper City in the Ghetto** 'cause it's like that all across the world. I'm gonna give it to 'em raw like that.

Are you 20 now?

B.G.:
19.

And you put out five albums at 19?

B.G.:
Really seven, including my five solos, plus my two with the Hot Boys. Plus I got another one I'm about to put out and another Hot Boys. Really like ten albums.

What goes through your mind when you're doing all this? How do you come up with all these lyrics?

B.G.:
I'm a Rapper. It's just in me. It's just in me. I just got talent. I thank the Lord for this.

How do you sleep?

B.G.:
Like any normal person. When I get tired, I go my ass to sleep.

Are you not restless? You're putting across everything that you want?

B.G.:
Yeah! No doubt.

What was the NOLA scene like before? There was Bounce music -

B.G.:
Yeah.

And then you came and took it to the next level?

B.G.:
Then Cash Money came and took it to the next level. It was Bounce music. Then they had Gangsta Bounce or whatever. Cash Money just came with straight gangsta shit, straight real like N.W.A type shit.

Why does everyone avoid mentioning No Limit?

B.G.:
We care not to discuss that. Who is No Limit? Never heard of 'em.

You came first with the Army, and then all of a sudden they're Soldiers.

B.G.:
Yeah.

You come first with Hot Boys, then all of a sudden they're Hot Boys.

B.G.:
You can answer that yourself. When one person comes with something, then somebody comes behind 'em with it, what you call that? A follower. They want to be like you. That's all I can see.

How come they were the first to put it across?

B.G.:
I don't know. Like I said, I care not to talk about them.

B.G. followed up **Chopper City In The Ghetto** with *Checkmate* on November 21, 2000, and then parted ways with Cash Money Records due to a financial dispute. Soon after he formed his very own label, Chopper City Records. Prior to this rumours had circulated that he and Turk had a stormy relationship with heroin. Livin' Legends was issued February 25, 2003. B.G. maintained a regular release schedule issuing one new album per year. Beginning with *Life After Cash Money* in 2004, *The Heat On The Streetz, Vol. 1* in 2005, and *The Heat On The Streetz, Vol. 2 (I Am What I Am)* in 2006, which debuted at #6 on the Billboard Top 200.

B.G. And The Chopper City Boyz dropped the **We Got This** album on February 27, 2007. It sold well enough to hit the Billboard Top 200 at #21 and became his first #1 on the Independent Album charts. He signed with Atlantic Records later the same year, thanks to T.I. In late 2007 news circulated that a Hot Boys reunion was in the works. A show was featuring B.G., Juvenile, Lil Wayne, and Mannie Fresh replacing the incarcerated Turk, was scheduled during NBA All-Star weekend in New Orleans for February 17, 2008. Unfortunately, before it got underway, three people were shot outside the venue, and the show cancelled.

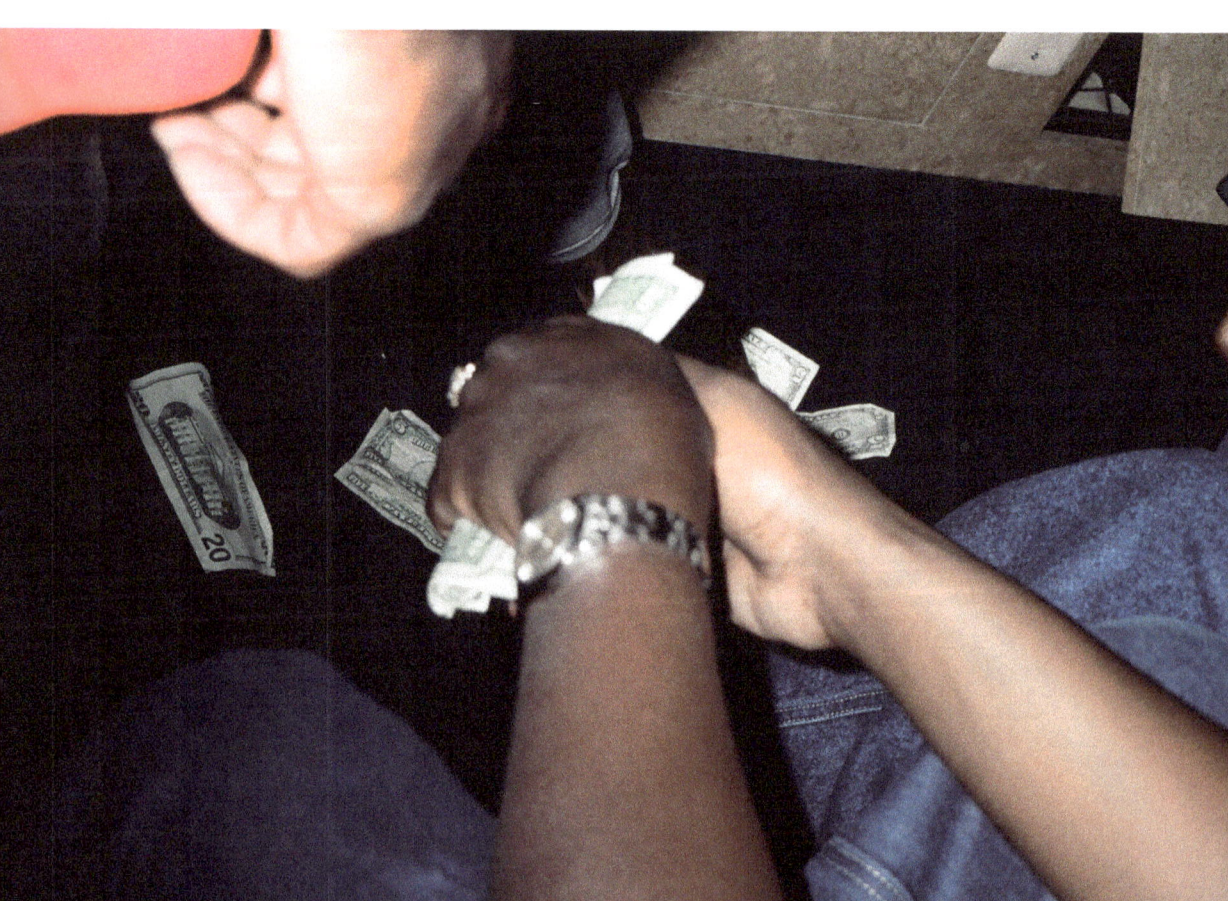

In 2008, B.G., Lil Wayne, and Juvenile recorded their first track together since 2001, "Ya Heard Me" featuring Cool & Dre and Trey Songz. B.G. & Chopper City Boyz released their second album, **Life In The Concrete Jungle**, on September 16, 2008. The solo album **Too Hood 2 Be Hollywood** was issued in late 2009. Mannie Fresh featured on the first single "My Hood", and "Back To The Money" features unexpected special guest appearances from Lil Wayne and Birdman.

B.G. was arrested on November 3, 2009, at a routine traffic stop and search when three guns, two of them stolen, loaded magazines, two extended clips, and drugs located in the vehicle, which was taken from an Alamo rental lot.

B.G. and Lil Boosie released a joint mixture titled 225 504 on June 7, 2010. B.G. quickly followed up with his own mixture release **Money Side: Murda Side** on July 8, 2010. His most recent album, Hollyhood, was issued by Rbc Records on October 5, 2010.

B.G. was sentenced to 14 years in prison for gun possession and witness tampering on July 18, 2012.

B.G. ALBUM DISCOGRAPHY

- **True Story** with Lil Wayne - July 28, 1995 (Cash Money Records)
- **Chopper City** - February 26, 1996 (Cash Money Records)
- **It's All On U, Vol. 1** - July 1, 1997 (Cash Money Records)
- **It's All On U, Vol. 2** - November 15, 1997 (Cash Money Records)
- **Chopper City In The Ghetto** - April 20, 1999 (Cash Money Records)
- **Checkmate** - November 21, 2000 (Cash Money Records)
- **Livin' Legend** - February 25, 2003 (Chopper City Records)
- **Life After Cash Money** - July 27, 2004 (Chopper City Records)
- **The Heart of Tha Streetz, Vol. 1** - May 24, 2005 (Chopper City Records)
- **The Heart of Tha Streetz, Vol. 2 (I Am What I Am)** - March 21, 2006 (Chopper City Records)
- **Too Hood 2 Be Hollywood** - December 8, 2009 (Chopper City Records)
- **Hollyhood** - October 5, 2010 (Rbc Records)

HOT BOYS

- **Get It How U Live!!** - October 28, 1997 (Cash Money Records)
- **Guerilla Warfare** - July 27, 1999 (Cash Money Records)
- **Let 'Em Burn** - March 25, 2003 (Cash Money Records)

B.G. AND THE CHOPPER CITY BOYZ

- **We Got This** - February 27, 2007 (Chopper City Records)
- **Life in the Concrete Jungle** - September 16, 2008 (Chopper City Records)

CHAPTER 4

I DON'T GET CAUGHT IN THE MIST

Juvenile was born Terius Gray, March 25, 1975.

Juvenile is the only Hot Boy to record music with another label before Cash Money Records. Instrumental in the creation of Bounce, he has recordings dating back to 1990, with his song "Bounce (For The Juvenile)" becoming a regional success in 1991.

Juvenile signed to New York City-based Warlock Records, owned by Adam Levy, the son of notorious music impresario Morris Levy (Google him), where he released the **Being Myself** album in 1995. Success in the South crickets everyone else, it generated the interest of Cash Money Records who took him into their bosom and immediately connected him with Mannie Fresh.

Solja Rags, his 1997 Cash Money Records debut, laid the foundation and hinted at what was to come. When **400 Degreez** arrived on the scene in November 1998, Juvenile set the world on fire and dominated radio, video and clubs on the strength of "Ha" and "Back That Azz Up" undeniably influencing the manner Southern Rap was received for decades to come selling over four million copies in the process.

What's the new album?

Juvenile:

The new album is talking about how we grew up. It's some more hood shit. I'm trying to let everybody know what we've been through and what I've been through to get to where I'm at now and talk about past life things. It's just some ghetto life shit.

Break it down.

Juvenile:

Shit, you know, how we used to hustle and shit; how we sold rocks and shit; how motherfuckers have to think when they out here. Especially when you in the Projects and shit you usually have a street mentality. Really what I'm talking about is I'm describing my neighbourhood and our G Code, just that. The way we dress; the way we talk, our language; the way we carry ourself in public and shit; what we like to do. That's what my album is about.

What's the Juvenile state of mind?

Juvenile:

Shit, I'm still on some hustling shit. I look at Rap like I used to look at the game. I'm a hustler.

You changed the Rap game. You and your clique has altered the whole Rap game.

Juvenile:

Well, I don't want to say we changed it. We brought it to us, and right now all eyes focused on us because we stayed working. Work ethics is the way of the Rap game. If you're not doing nothing and you're sitting on your ass, and you expect your album to sell it ain't gonna happen. You can have an album full of hits. If you ain't working that hit, you ain't shit. That goes for this shit right here: interviews, promotions; letting the public see you going out there to every ghetto, or going out there to the malls and shit all over the country; being on TV, the videos, this movie. That's what makes us. That's why the game come to us. We hard workers.

How did you link up with the brothers?

Juvenile:
I always did know 'em. I was doing my thing before the Company started, and by me being out the same hood, and so close around 'em, it wasn't hard for them to put a hand on me and talk to me. And the first opportunity I got to do something with 'em; I did it 'cause I was caught up in a contract. So when I got released, I came straight to Cash Money 'cause that's where I wanted to be anyway.

What attracted you to them?

Juvenile:
Shit, the music! Mannie Fresh! I like the beats. Music comes first. If you want to make a hit song, the music is fifty percent, and the rap is fifty percent.

So Mannie had a name for himself out here for a while?

Juvenile:
Mannie always was - Mannie was a legend a long time ago down here. That was like our only entertainer down here as far as music is concerned. He always took stars that was the shit. The words didn't count. It was all really on him. His beats made motherfuckers stars, and along comes me a talented motherfucker that can rap and that was able to complement his beats. That's where the chemistry flow got good at, and that's what made us get to where we at now.

Talk about the background of the NOLA scene. Did you come from Bounce music?

Juvenile:
I am Bounce, man! I'm the inventor of Bounce, so I don't come from Bounce music. Bounce music comes from me, and everybody followed behind me because I was the trendsetter. We like club music. We uptempo beats and shit. Pac used to rap on uptempo shit and slow tempo shit, but me generally, I like hype shit. I don't like no slow drag it down ass music. Like for instance, if you go out to a club and a motherfucker cut on slow songs they gonna get just that reaction out of the crowd. That's why we basically - Me personally, I like uptempo shit. I like motherfuckers to snap they head and get wild and cut shit up on my music.

Who is in the crew?

Juvenile:
Me, Wayne, Turk, B.G., Mannie Fresh, Baby, Suga Slim. Our roster goes on. But we all talented, we all talented in our own special way. All of us got something different with us. Baby kind of like an entrepreneur, he comes along, and he tries his best to keep us focused on what we doing and bring out the real inner talent that we got because we used to be holding back on a lot of shit. He was like you need to do that more; you need to use this melody; you need to talk about this more. And that's how we work.

With all the stuff going on around you how do you keep your eyes on the music?

Juvenile:
I got faith in God, that's where everything comes from. I'm well blessed, and I acknowledge that I'm blessed, and I take full responsibility on my responsibilities. If I got a problem I deal with it myself, and that's what keeps me focused, and I keep my people straight. I break bread. Just 'cause I'm rich, or just 'cause I'm making money don't mean I'm gonna forget about my people, and that's what makes me tick.

How is life different now than when you were hustlin'?

Juvenile:
Life ain't different, life ain't different for me 'cause I never really got caught up. I never was a follower. I always have been a leader, and all I had to do was use my inner talent 'cause I always was talented with Rap. I use my inner talent and stay focused on what I was trying to do, and now I'm making money from it. That's all I want.

Give me some lessons you have learned.

Juvenile:
Shit! A big lesson I learned was speak when you're spoken to. Mind your business. That was my biggest lesson. I used to dip into motherfuckers business and pass my opinion where it wasn't needed. I got a little smarter. Then I learned how to take care of my people and stay closer with my people than what I used to do. That was the only changes I needed to make. To take care of myself, put myself - put God first, myself and God first, and that helped me out a lot.

What role does God play in your success?

Juvenile:
God plays a role in everybody success 'cause you give, and you take, and it's on you if you don't want to give your dues back, your ten percent, or whatever. Me personally, I haven't been the best motherfucker maybe as far as going to Church and saying my prayers all the time, but I do know there is a God because I'm blessed being. I used to live right there, and drugs tore my family up, and I brought my family back together. I said my prayers, the Lord blessed me and here I am.

How ill does it get in the Magnolia?

Juvenile:
It ain't the Projects; it's the people in it. It can be a motherfucker off the outside come in here and commit a murder. Murder is murder no matter where it happens at; This Project is cause for crime because it's so many poor people. People broke, man. Motherfuckers struggling. If you gave everybody in this Project a million dollars a piece, I don't think you would have crime back here. It's a money thing and everybody trying to get it. If you have at

Juvenile:

God play a role in everybody success 'cause you give and you take, and it's on you if you don't want to give your dues back, your ten percent, or whatever. Me personally, I haven't been the best motherfucker maybe as far as going to Church and saying my prayers all the time but I do know there is a God because I'm blessed being. I used to live right there and drugs tore my family up, and I kind of brought my family back together. I said my prayers, the Lord blessed me and here I am.

How ill does it get in the Magnolia?

Juvenile:

It ain't the Projects, it's the people in it. It can be a motherfucker off the outside come in here and commit a murder. Murder is murder no matter where it happen at. This Project is cause for crime because it's so many poor people. People broke, man. Motherfuckers struggling. If you gave everybody in this Project a million dollars a piece I don't think you would have crime back here. It's a money thing and everybody trying to get it. If you have at least $20 000, and the next man don't have it, and you out there with it and maybe he feels like he can take it to do what he got to do. He gonna do what he got to do, so that's life.

No matter how hard you work for your money, there's ten guys working harder to take it from you.

Juvenile:
Yeah, but that was as far as the money is concerned. It ain't so much of the money. Motherfuckers want to be seen. Motherfuckers want to be in that spotlight, even if it means being in the spotlight for a minute. They'll put they life on the line to be in the spotlight, and I've been through it. I feel they pain. Motherfuckers struggling.

What have you seen growing up here?

Juvenile:
Shit, I seen everything. That type of shit I'd rather not even talk about what I've seen. I would be a Rat if I sit here and tell you what I seen. I've seen a lot. I've done did things and all that, but that ain't nothin' to be saying in an interview.

Who came first, you or No Limit?

Juvenile:
I don't want to discuss that. Go to the next question.

You mention **The Young and the Restless** in many interviews. Do you watch that all the time?

Juvenile:
Nah, I don't watch that shit all the time. I just used to be into it because I didn't have nothing to do. I ain't have no source of income. I sit my ass inside, everybody wanted to watch it, so I watched it, and I started liking the shit.

What do you want people to know about Juvenile?

Juvenile:
I'm human, that's all I want. I'm human just like everybody else. I'm human. I'm just a Black man trying to get my shit right. Not worrying about what the next man doing, trying to stay focused on my family and eat, that's it.

What can people learn off *G-Code*?

Juvenile:
You won't learn shit if you don't know what I went through. If you can't feel it, you ain't going to learn shit. All you gonna learn about is what I went through. My whole album is focused on street life and the way - like I said, the way we talk, the way we grew up. The things we went through and the struggles that each and every man has. You can get street knowledge from me. You can get a lot of street knowledge from me, but it's on you. Life is what you make it. If you want to be a thug and you listen to it for the wrong things that might be the perfect song for you to listen to. If you want to be a smart motherfucker and stay away from that shit and try to make something out of your life you can learn from me.

I try to make a motherfucker enjoy they-self. I try to put the fun back into Rap because Rap started getting boring and everybody want to talk about what they got and all that shit. That's cool; I do it. We do it here, but I'm a street motherfucker I can only talk about what I know about.

Any tracks for people to look out?

Juvenile:
Everything. My whole album, man. My whole album. My shit sells.

There is a difference between **Solja Rags** and **400 Degreez**.

Juvenile:
It's all uptempo music though; still catering to the crowds, the clubs and shit. Like I said, if I go in a club and they cut on some slow shit I'm gonna lean on the wall. If they cut on some hype shit, I might stand up. I ain't no rout it, rout it, motherfucker. I might stand up. If I'm with the thugs and then they had a few drinks, I'm gonna get buck, but if they cut up some slow shit that's what they gonna get.

What's your favourite drink?

Juvenile:
Hennessy; VSOP, XO. As long as it's cognac and it's good quality grain I want it.

What do you eat?

Juvenile:
I eat Black people food, ghetto food.

What's that?

Juvenile:
Fuck, everything they cook in the ghetto. I don't eat no chitlins or none of that shit. I eat gumbo, smothered pork chops, steaks, all that shit. You know, one thing in the ghetto, man. Black man makes a meal out of anything. Momma gets in the kitchen and whip up anything and make you lick your fingers.

What have you seen while touring and travelling?

Juvenile:

I don't get caught in the mist, man. I don't get caught in the mist. I don't pay attention to motherfuckers. I focus on what I'm doing, and I go lock up in my room. It's all business. On the road, it's not smart to be getting out there and chilling and hanging and making friends 'cause them same motherfuckers might be trying to pull something off or want to see where you're head at, so I don't give them nothing to see. I don't give them nothing. I'm like a motherfucking shill when I'm out of town. You don't know nothing; you ain't know nothing. You don't know nothing about me, and you won't know nothing extra about me, but I can put on a show. That's all you gonna know.

What about women?

Juvenile:

They come a dime a dozen, man. I don't entertain that shit. I like women. Women support me. I like 'em. Fuck, I ain't no gay. I get my fuck on here and there but I ain't lovin' them hoes. I got two children, man. I don't fuck with some of that shit. I'm trying to feed my family.

Can women be trusted?

Juvenile:

I mean, I ain't gonna sit here and say every woman in the world evil 'cause I got a momma, so fuckin' right women can be trusted. Certain ones. It all depends on who you are. You might put your trust in a woman. You might have a good woman that you don't trust, and she might be the perfect motherfucker for you, and you might go fuck with this little two dollar ass hoe, and she might get you locked up, get you set up, get you killed. It's not smart to have a whole lot of hoes. Two or three here and there are cool. A whole lot, that's like you can't watch everything. You don't know what you can't see.

***

Tha G-Code arrived one month later and quickly sold over 2 million copies. Project English followed in the summer of 2001 and sold over 1 million copies. Juvenile left Cash Money Records and formed the group UTP with Wacko, Skip, Corey Cee, Soulja Slim and Young Buck. Orpheus Music released the self-produced ***Juvenile Presents UTP Playas: The Compilation*** in October 2002.

The double-disc compilation ***Juvenile Presents Street Stories: UTP Playas & Skip*** released in May 2003. Juvenile then renegotiated with Cash Money Records, who paid him a reported $4 000 000 for the ***Juve The Great*** album.

50 Cent recruited Wacko, Skip and Young Buck and Buck joined G-Unit. Soulja Slim was murdered on November 26, 2003, and Corey Cee quit. Juvenile, Wacko & Skip signed a deal with Rap-A-Lot Records/Asylum Records.

Juve The Great was released in December 2003 and sold over 1 million copies highlighted by a two-week run at #1 on the Billboard singles chart for "Slow Motion" featuring late NOLA legend, Soulja Slim.

UTP's ***The Beginning of the End...*** was released in May 2004. The single "Nolia Clap" crossed over resulting in the release of the Nolia Clap EP in November 2004.

In 2005, Juvenile signed with Atlantic Records where he maintained his solo career and launched his very own UTP label in fine form with the "Nolia Clap" remix. His Atlantic Records debut, ***Reality Check***, came on March 6, 2006, and became his first and only Billboard #1 album, though it ironically sold fewer copies than his Cash Money Records releases.

By the time his next album, ***Cocky & Confident***, was issued in December 2009, the music landscape had shifted, and artists that grew up soaking in the sounds of Juvenile were now leading the pack. ***Beast Mode*** came in 2010, 2012 brought ***Rejuvenation***, and The ***Fundamentals*** from 2014 rounds out his solo catalogue, to date.

Juvenile has had his share of run-ins with the law, however nothing that landed him in jail. An assault charge on the barber who bootlegged his music, paternity and child support on the domestic front, and marijuana.

Juvenile signed a new deal with Cash Money Records in October 2014. A new album is imminent.

By the time his next album, **Cocky & Confident**, was issued in December 2009, the music landscape had shifted, and artists that grew up soaking in the sounds of Juvenile were now leading the pack. Beast Mode came in 2010, 2012 brought **Rejuvenation**, and **The Fundamentals** from 2014 rounds out his solo catalogue, to date.

Juvenile has had his share of run-ins with the law, however nothing that landed him in jail. An assault charge on the barber who bootlegged his music, paternity and child support on the domestic front, and marijuana.

Juvenile signed a new deal with Cash Money Records in October 2014. A new album is imminent.

JUVENILE ALBUM DISCOGRAPHY

- **Being Myself** - February 7, 1995 (Warlock)
- **Solja Rags** - May 13, 1997 (Cash Money Records)
- **400 Degreez** - November 9, 1998 (Cash Money Records)
- **Tha G-Code** - December 13, 1999 (Cash Money Records)
- **Project English** - August 21, 2001 (Cash Money Records)
- **Juve The Great** - December 23, 2003 (Cash Money Records)
- **Reality Check** - March 7, 2006 (Atlantic/UPT)
- **Cocky & Confident** - December 1, 2009 (UTP/E1)
- **Beast Mode** - July 6, 2010 (UTP/E1)
- **Rejuvenation** - June 19, 2012 (Rap-A-Lot/Young Empire)
- **The Fundamentals** - February 18, 2014 (Rap-A- Lot)

HOT BOYS

- **Get It How U Live!!** - October 28, 1997 (Cash Money Records)
- **Guerilla Warfare** - July 27, 1999 (Cash Money Records)
- **Let 'Em Burn** - March 25, 2003 (Cash Money Records)

UTP

- **Juvenile Presents UTP Playas: The Compilation** - October 8, 2002 (Orpheus Records)
- **Juvenile Presents Street Stories: UTP Playas & Skip** - May 27, 2003 (Orpheus Records)
- **The Beginning Of The End** - May 18, 2004 (Rap-A-Lot/Asylum)
- **Nolia Clap EP** - November 23, 2004 (Rap-A-Lot/ Asylum)

CHAPTER 5
I'M GONNA LIVE AND DIE IN THIS HERE

Lil Wayne was born Dwayne Michael Carter, Jr., September 27, 1982.

Lil' Wayne entered the Rap game at the age of 9 and signed with Cash Money Records at 10. An only child living in the Projects, life moved at a rapid pace as his responsibilities increased. Though he excelled in school and became an Honours student, to care for his mother his after-school program placement was hustlin' on the block.

He recorded his first Cash Money Records album, **True Story**, at the age of 12. When he went by Lil Doogie, in a group called the BG'z with B.G. In an unfortunate accident, he shot himself in the chest with his mother's 9 mm at the age of 12, and shortly after that took an extended leave of absence from the music business. He marked his return to Cash Money Records at the age of 14 and then dropped out of school in 1996 to pursue a music career full-time.

In 1997, Lil Wayne tasted success for the first time on albums by B.G., Juvenile, Big Tymers, and the first Hot Boys album, **Get It How U Live!!**. His major break came with his guest shot on Juvenile's "Back That Azz Up" that dominated the spring of 1999. When his long-awaited solo debut, **Tha Block Is Hot**, finally arrived the first week of November 1999, it sold 250 000 copies its first week and entered the Billboard charts at #3.

***

What is Lil Wayne?

Lil Wayne:
Real. I could describe it in one word, real. Straight from the street, the block all I know, ain't gonna give you nothing else but the block.

What was it like growing up?

Lil Wayne:
Like every other nigga out the hood growing up. You got to get that cheddah, that's all it was about, cheddah.; hitting the block, scramblin', hustlin'; raw. Why is it so raw out here?

Lil Wayne:
I don't know, man. Can't tell you why. I guess that's how niggas wanna ball. It's raw everywhere, man. Niggas wanna ball 'cause I know I do.

How does Lil Wayne ball?

Lil Wayne:
I'm ballin' out of control now. We got platinum albums. I'm ballin' now. Do what I want to do now. But back in the G, I had to do what I could do. Ballin'!

What did you do to get over back in the day?

Lil Wayne:
I told ya; hustlin', scramblin', whatever I could.

How did you link up with Cash Money?

Lil Wayne:
A nigga out of my hood. One of they former Rappers name Lil Slim. He was from my hood, from the same block, Apple and Eagle, he put me down.

Are you sixteen now?

Lil Wayne:
Yeah.

How long have you been doing this?

Lil Wayne:
Too long. Been doing this since I was nine. Been with Cash Money since I was ten. I'm thuggin'. I'm gonna live and die in this here.

What's your role in the Hot Boys?

Lil Wayne:
Be me, Lil Weezy holding it down. The youngest got to hold it down. Hold down my part, concentrate from the block.

How is your album going?

Lil Wayne:
Wonderful.

Where is it at now? Is it selling?

Lil Wayne:
What you think? 250 000 the first week.

Why are people looking at Cash Money these days?

Lil Wayne:
Why? 'Cause we got the game on lock and we lost the key, and they calling us to see if they can find the key but we can't, so it's locked permanently.

Will this will go on forever?

Lil Wayne:
'Til we find the key, and I don't think we looking for it at all, believe that.

As a young entrepreneur why the record game and not something else?

Lil Wayne:
'Cause this what I slipped into. 'Cause if it was something else it might be something raw, so this what I flipped into. This is what I want to do, and it happened for me, so that's why.

There's a Cash Money slang. Can you break that down?

Lil Wayne:
I mean, ain't no Cash Money slang. It's an uptown slang; it's a New Orleans thing. Everybody from New Orleans talk like how we talk. Our slang is conversation down here but it's slang across the world, they're getting used to it. Its just natural habit, we can't even leave that. We can't leave that if we try.

What's your album **Tha Block Is Hot** all about?

Lil Wayne:
The street, real. What go on and what could go on. On the block or the street. It's just real.

Is there a Lil Wayne state of mind?

Lil Wayne:
Yeah, my state of mind, man. Young nigga hustlin' tryin' to get it, ya feel me. If a nigga in my way I'm a split him just the way I was taught; Kill 'em all.

What did you see growing up over here?

Lil Wayne:
I seen too much. I witnessed too much. I've been through too much. Seen a lot of shit. Everything there is to see. That's what I saw.

What are your earliest memories?

Lil Wayne:
Shit, everything. It ain't nothing 'cause it's so natural. Ain't nothing to be unusual. Killings, that ain't unusual no more. We the murder capital of the world. I saw too many of them, ain't nothing. Snitches. How it can get you crossed up, how it can get you killed. I done talked too much and it's regular. If I was still on the block, I'd still be seeing it going through it.

The people you grew up with are still in it?

Lil Wayne
Yeah, but my niggas that I grew up with are in jail, so … I don't know about all the rest of them niggas. They still doing their thing.

Do you keep in touch with people?

Lil Wayne:
Mmmmhmmm. I holler.

What do you want to put across?

Lil Wayne:
What's my point? That the block is hot. It's real, so if you playin' - If you on the block already you know where I'm coming from. If you plan on going to the block, you know what to expect, and if you stand away from the block do so.

What have you seen touring around? What's going through your mind when you're travelling?

Lil Wayne:
I be lovin' it, it be cool. I feel that. It don't be exciting me though. I'm more a natural nigga; I don't get too excited. It be cool though, I ain't trippin'.

What do you hope to accomplish in life?

Lil Wayne:
I accomplished what I wanted to do, be a Rapper, feel me, and be a real Rapper. I'm a Rapper. I'm an accomplished Rapper. I ain't got too many new goals. I might … I don't know, sell 10 million records, 30 million records. What do you do with the money you bring in?

Lil Wayne:
Putting it up 'cause you never know I might have to go back to the block if something shaky. That's what I'm doing with it.

You saving it?

Lil Wayne:
Yep. I'm buying stuff here and there 'cause I got to get my shine on.

Is it essential to floss?

Lil Wayne:

Too important. In New Orleans very important.

Why?

Lil Wayne:

'Cause that's what this city based on; shine and bling bling. All that stuff.

Do you buy your own or does the company buy you everything?

Lil Wayne:

Nah, I buy my own.

Is there one jeweller Cash Money goes?

Lil Wayne:

Yeah, something like that but we all go to our own. Some of us drift off to other ones. There is one of 'em that we all work with.

Why does no one in your organisation talk about No Limit?

Lil Wayne:

I don't know if I'm ignoring this one.

What is your relationship with Mannie Fresh?

Lil Wayne:

He like a big brother, man. Nigga crazy, man. That nigga the goofiest nigga on earth. That nigga is crazy.

Who has been the most inspirational figure for you?

Lil Wayne:

Rabbit, Baby and Slim. My daddy Rabbit, he deceased, and Baby and Slim, they all put me on my game. Let me know how to look at life.

How do you look at life?

Lil Wayne:

We ain't promised tomorrow, so whatever you want to do, do it. Whatever in your fate go get it. Anything in your way move it. That's how I look at it.

Do you run into a lot of adversity?

Lil Wayne:
I don't know what the fuck that is. What is that?

People against you -

Lil Wayne:
Oh, oh, oh ... I can say I run into it but by me not giving a fuck about it I don't care, so I don't know if I do or don't 'cause I don't care, whatever. I mean, if they're against me let 'em be against me. Get in my way I'm gonna move you. Plain and simple. They could be on the sideline hanging, but if you in the middle of the field prepare to play the game.

What is the game?

Lil Wayne:
Run or get ran over.

What happens if someone crosses Lil Wayne?

Lil Wayne:
They get crossed out, and that's if they cross me they better cross me out. If you gonna get in my way, push me down to make me fall to where I never get up 'cause if I get back up I'm a move you. Like I say, I was taught never give up, and anything in your way move it.

How do you stay ahead of everyone else? There's a lot of people who think like that, but your actions and reactions put you over.

Lil Wayne:
Live by it and die by it. Live by what I was told. A lot of people think like that. A lot of people don't mean that. I mean that, feel me.

Has it ever come to that?

Lil Wayne:
Many a time. That's why I'm where I'm at now, and I don't think I'm in no bad position.

Were the Police always after you and trying to put you down?

Lil Wayne:
That's gonna be forever and a day. Police gonna hate no matter what but like I say … I mean, they don't get in my way, but that's just something. That something that gonna be there forever, man. Police don't want to see a nigga do nothing anyway. Fuck 'em - in the ass.

Why do they hate on you?

Lil Wayne:
They ain't hating on me. They been doing this shit way before my time. Been hating four hundred years ago, been hating.

Is it worse down here?

Lil Wayne:
It ain't bad down here. It ain't bad as I know it is in other States and stuff. It ain't bad down here. It's cool. They fuck over you around here, but they don't fuck over you like they do in L.A. and shit like that. It ain't that serious. Niggas down here crazy, man. You have a lot of Police getting found dead if that shit was going on down here.

Does the heat play a role in the sound of Cash Money? How hot it gets in the summer and the humidity?

Lil Wayne:
I don't know. I ain't never been asked that. It play a role in my bling bling, with the sunbeam on my bling bling, that's it. We get our shine on mostly in the summer. That's when our rims can shine. The summer a lot of niggas get killed. A lot of niggas get killed in the summer down here. That's the kind of role it is, that's what the summer bring; death. It be hot! You know how niggas get when it's hot. Nigga be needing that money. Drought might come through the summer. Nigga do whatever!

How do you deal with women?

Lil Wayne:
If I like 'em I ... Like 'em, love 'em and leave 'em. I don't know. They come - If I like what I see if I deal with 'em. After I deal with 'em they dealt with. They could dash.

No relationship, no trust?

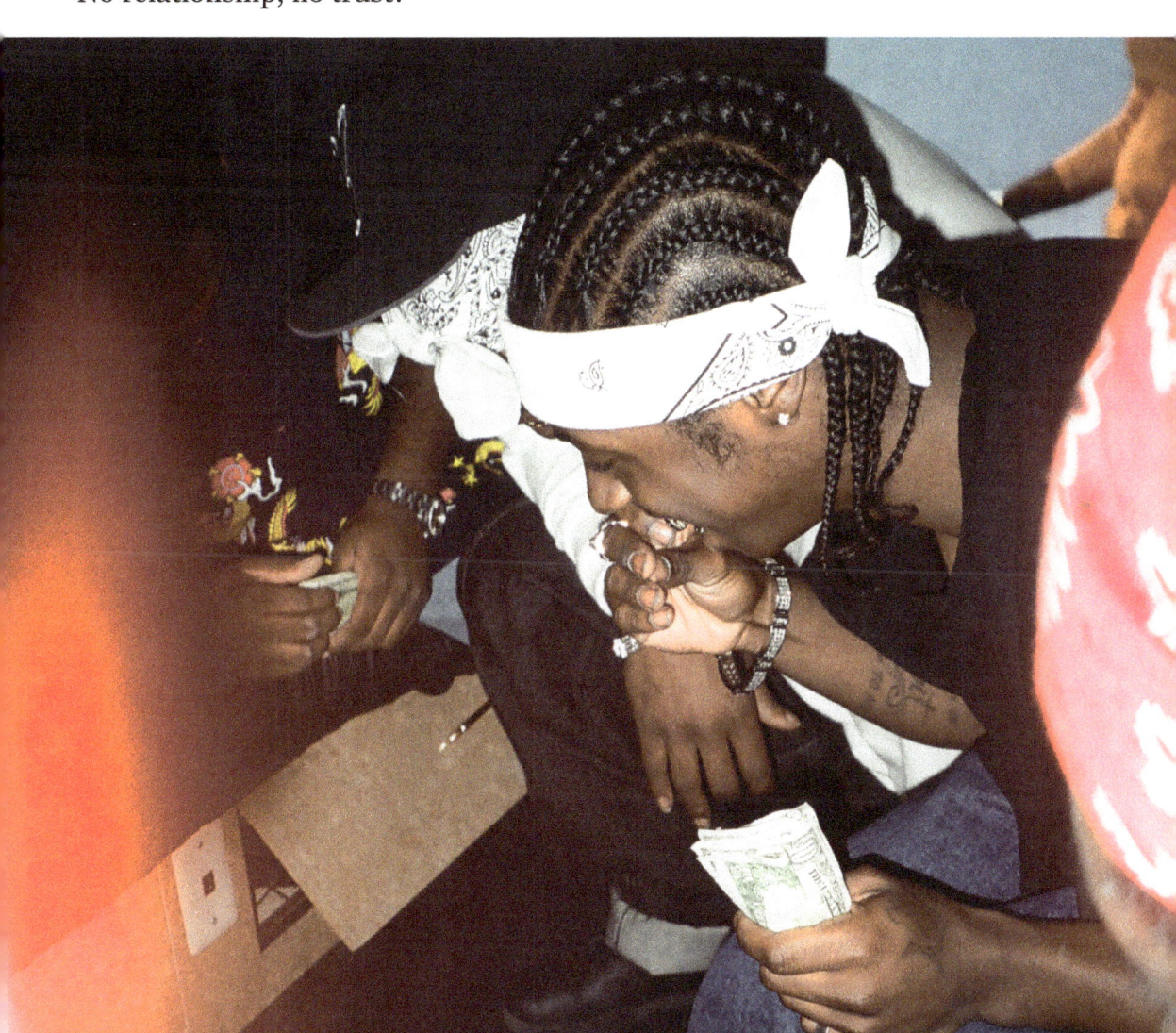

Lil Wayne:
Got somebody already, so I'm chillin.' Any other outside of her ain't no relationship or no trust just-just a raw thirty minutes of 'em, and they could skit. Other than that wodie gonna be there.

Do you have any kids?

Lil Wayne:
Yeah, I got one. I got a little girl.

How old is she?

Lil Wayne:
She about to be a year on the 29th.

How did that change you?

Lil Wayne:
It ain't changed me too much. It just made my responsibility level higher, that's it ... I've been a little man, feel me? I was on the block doing my thing. Once you start that you a man. You start handling stuff like that you're a man, so I've been a little man, so it was cool. I just got to take care of more shit.

How early did life start on the block?

Lil Wayne:
11! 11, 12. I had to get it on.

No school? Were you out there just slangin'?

Lil Wayne:
Nah, I went to school 'cause I couldn't let my people ... I'm an only child. It ain't like I got brothers and sisters for my momma to worry about. She was only worrying about me, and I didn't want to bust her brain letting her know I'm hustling, so I went to school, got good grades and everything. But after school, come home, drop them books, get out that uniform and hit the block; let's get this paper.

What's next for Lil Wayne?

Lil Wayne:

This movie. We got Juvenile album about to drop; I'll be on there. Hot Boys about to come back out. Big Tymers, I'm all over there. Everything with an S on it you gonna see Lil Wayne. Anything Cash Money got coming up. They got this new tour coming up with the Ruff Ryders in January, which will be the biggest tour of the year.

Hot Boys coming the same way, or are you flipping it?

Lil Wayne:

I ain't gonna say we comin' the same way. We just comin' the best way we know how, feel me? Another nigga might be like that's the same way. Another nigga might be like that's different, that's tight. We just comin'! We still burnin' shit. We still choppin' shit. It's raw.

You were on Cash Money before the Universal deal.

Lil Wayne:

Way before the Universal deal.

What're the changes?

Lil Wayne:

We can't drop album after album like we used to. We used to drop a different album every month. Every month we had a different album, every two months. We can't drop, we can't do that. Got to wait. We getting it to where we could do that though. More work. Independent, you used to do what you want to do when you want to do it. Now you got to do what we have to do when it comes.

Do you come with your concepts?

Lil Wayne:

Yeah.

What concepts are you dealing with now?

Lil Wayne:

My concepts like I'm still on the block, ya feel me. Thankfully, I'm a just thug forever, and when they stop loving my style 'cause you know everybody have a page that turn. When they turn the page on me, I'm still gonna be on that same page doing what I do. If they turn it back, I'm gonna be doing what I do love it or leave it. I ain't changing. My concepts gonna be the same. It might come out differently, but they still gonna be the same.

How do you keep your mind on the music with everything going on around you?

Lil Wayne:
'Cause it's what got me here. That's why I don't let what's going on around me bother me. This movie, I do that, but that ain't what got me here. I ain't get here … I wasn't no actor; I ain't no actor. So I do that, I put twenty percent into the movie, but I'm putting the rest of it in Rap. I mean, this what got me here. I'm a Rapper, gonna be a Rapper, feel me?

Is there anything else?

Lil Wayne:
I'm cool.

***

Lil Wayne is quite possibly the most prolific Rapper of all-time.

Lights Out followed the platinum-certified ***Tha Block Is Hot*** in late 2000 and achieved gold sales status. 500 Degreez came in the summer of 2002 and duplicated the feat.

In 2002, Lil Wayne formed Sqad Up with Gudda Gudda, Nut da Kid, T-Streets, Raw Dizzy, Young Yo, Fee Banks, and Super Branco. Together the crew recorded and released 6 ***SQ*** mixtapes in 2002 and 2003, and Lil Wayne added his first solo mixtape, ***Da Drought,*** for good measure.

2004 was another busy year in the studio with two mixtape releases, ***Da Drought 2*** and ***The Prefix***, and the first album in his acclaimed ***Tha Carter*** series.

Lil Wayne was named President of Cash Money Records and launched his imprint, Young Money Entertainment. That winter brought ***The Suffix*** mixtape, ***Tha Carter II*** album, and the first release in the classic ***Gangsta Grillz*** mixtape series with DJ Drama, ***Dedication: Gangsta Grillz***, one week later on December 13, 2005.

    2006 was perhaps his busiest year in the studio. Lil Wayne maintained a constant pace with nine mixtape releases. ***Dedication 2: Gangsta Grillz.*** The introduction to his Young Money label and crew on ***Young Money: The Mixtape Vol. 1 & Vol. 2. Lil Weezy Ana; The Carter Files;*** two Reebok sponsored ***The W. Carter Collection 1 & 2; Blow***: The ***I Can't Feel My Face Prequel*** with Juelz Santana; a proper collaboration album with Birdman a.k.a. Baby, ***Like Father, Like Son***, and its mixtape Lil Wayne, Birdman & DJ Khaled - ***The Carter 2: Part 2 Like Father, Like Son***.

    On July 22, 2007, Lil Wayne was arrested inside his tour bus by New York City Police and charged with one count of criminal weapons possession and one charge of unlawful possession of a loaded weapon. The whole situation was shady as the Police claimed they smelled marijuana to gain access to the bus, which they then searched before arresting him.

Lil Wayne was quiet on the mixtape front in 2007 with only one release, though it was colossal. **Da Drought 3** approached two hours of music and included guest shots by a cross-section of top artists, including Jay-Z, Beyonce, Kanye West, Nas, Lauryn Hill, Rick Ross, T.I., Ciara, R. Kelly, Swizz Beatz, Cam'Ron, Young Jeezy, and the list goes on.

In high demand, He stayed busy in the studio delivering top-shelf special guest appearances on singles for Jay-Z, Chris Brown, DJ Khaled, Fat Joe, Lloyd, Playaz Circle, Wyclef, Birdman, Little Brother, Kanye West, and Enrique Iglesias.

His fan base multiplied and demand for the **Tha Carter III** increased exponentially as it was pushed back several times. A few tracks leaked on unofficial mixtapes, and on Christmas Day 2007, **The Leak EP** rewarded them with a five-song taste of what was to come.

Tha Carter III finally released in the summer of 2008, and it exceeded the expectations of even his most hardcore fans. The album went on to win four Grammy Awards, including Best Rap Album and Best Rap Song for "Lollipop." Lil Wayne was also nominated for 12 BET Awards in 2008 and took home 8 of them. **Tha Carter III** became the top-selling record of the year with sales of over 3 million copies, and on November 11, 2008, Lil Wayne became the first Hip-Hop artist to perform at the Country Music Association Awards, playing "All Summer Long" alongside Kid Rock. Not a man to rest on his laurels, Lil Wayne dropped **Dedication 3: Gangsta Grillz** in December.

In 2009, Lil Wayne stretched out and tested the waters as a Sports commentator on ESPN. His raps were in such demand that his next mixtape, No Ceilings, leaked before its official release. It is notable for the inclusion of Young Money artists Nicki Minaj and Tyga. The We Are Young Money compilation album arrived Christmas week. Lil Wayne performs on every track with superstars Drake and Nicki Minaj appearing on four-track each.

In 2009, Lil Wayne stretched out and tested the waters as a Sports commentator on ESPN. His raps were in such demand that his next mixtape, **No Ceilings**, leaked before its official release. It is notable for the inclusion of Young Money artists Nicki Minaj and Tyga. The We Are Young Money compilation album arrived Christmas week. Lil Wayne performs on every track with superstars Drake and Nicki Minaj appearing on four-track each.

The Rebirth album arrived in February 2010 with a mix of Rock and Hip- Hop. The critics hate it, but it still sold over 500 000 copies and was certified gold. Lil Wayne was sentenced to jail for his July 22, 2007 charges, and began to serve his term March 8 at New York City's notorious jail complex, Rikers Island, on the East River. The special ***I Am Not A Human Being*** album arrived on his 28th birthday and landed at #1 on the Billboard charts.

Lil Wayne was released from prison after serving eight months on November 4. Lil Wayne scrapped his work on ***Tha Carter IV*** and began from scratch. The ***Sorry 4 The Wait*** mixtape was issued in July 2011, and ***Tha Carter IV*** finally came on August 29, 2011. It sold almost 1 million copies its first week and entered the Billboard charts at #1.

2012 was a quiet year with only one mixtape release, ***Dedication 4: Gangsta Grillz***, in September. On October 25, 2012, Lil Wayne's private jet, bound for Los Angeles, made an emergency landing in Texas due to an in-flight seizure, and again in Louisiana the following day as the flight resumed its course. He was hospitalised, again, on Mach 12, 2013, following another seizure, and spent six days in the critical care unit. It revealed that Lil Wayne had epilepsy, had suffered seizures for many years, and that combined with his use of codeine his body had broken down. On November 22, 2012, Lil Wayne announced that ***Tha Carter V*** would be his final album.

I Am Not A Human Being II arrived in March 2013, to reviews as mixed as its Hip-Hop and Rock music and entered the Billboard charts at #2. Lil Wayne participated on the Young Money issued ***Rich Gang*** compilation released in July 2013. **Dedication 5: Gangsta Grillz** came in September 2013.

The second Young Money compilation album, **Young Money: Rise Of An Empire,** was issued in March 2014 with Lil Wayne appearing on three songs. Fed up with multiple delays in his ***Tha Carter V*** album, Lil Wayne headed to Cash Money Records hometown nemesis, Master P and No Limit, and recorded "Power" with Master P, Gangsta and Ace B of Money Mafia.

Lil Wayne's ***Sorry 4 The Wait 2*** mixtape dropped on January 20, 2015. On January 28, He filed a $51 million lawsuit against Birdman and Cash Money Records. For delaying the release of ***Tha Carter V***, and failure to pay him monies on the success of Young Money Entertainment artists Drake, Nicki Minaj, and Tyga. In addition to advance and delivery monies for ***Tha Carter V.***

Then, to shake things up further, the ***Free Weezy Album*** came as an exclusive release on Jay-Z's TIDAL streaming service on Independence Day, July 4, and was streamed over 10 million times its first week.

Lil Wayne suffered two seizures on June 13, 2016, and his private jet made an emergency landing in Omaha where he was hospitalised, after reportedly drinking three 16-ounce bottles of codeine in a Milwaukee nightclub.

Lil Wayne directed a hearty "Fuck Cash Money" to those assembled at his second annual ***Lil Weezyana Fest*** homecoming show in New Orleans on August 27, 2016. Following the event, he donated its pop up skate park to New Orleans skate park, ***Parasite***.

On September 3, 2016, he issued a series of statements concerning the release on his Twitter account.

"I AM NOW DEFENSELESS AND mentally DEFEATED & I leave gracefully and thankful I luh my fanz but I'm dun"

"ain't lookin for sympathy, just serenity" and "I'm good y'all don't trip."

One week later, Lil Wayne released a new song "Grateful", featuring Gudda Gudda, commenting on the situation with Birdman and Cash Money Records. On September 23, he dropped the theme song for a new sports show hosted by Skip Bayless and Shannon Sharpe on Fox Sports 1, "No Mercy".

Lil Wayne continues to fight for his freedom from Cash Money Records.

LIL WAYNE ALBUM DISCOGRAPHY

- **Real Story** with B.G. - July 28, 1995 (Cash Money Records)
- **Tha Block Is Hot** - November 2, 1999 (Cash Money Records)
- **Lights Out** - December 19, 2000 (Cash Money Records)
- **500 Degreez** - July 23, 2002 (Cash Money Records)
- **Tha Carter** - June 29, 2004 (Cash Money Records)
- **Tha Carter II** - December 6, 2005 (Cash Money Records)
- **Like Father, Like Son** with Birdman - October 31, 2006 (Cash Money Records)
- **The Leak (EP)** - December 25, 2007 (Cash Money Records)
- **Tha Carter III** - June 10, 2008 (Cash Money Records)
- **Rebirth** - February 10, 2010 (Cash Money Records/Young Money Records)
- **I Am Not A Human Being** - September 27, 2010 (Cash Money Records/Young Money Records)
- **Tha Carter IV** - August 29, 2011 (Cash Money
- Records/Young Money Records)
- **I Am Not A Human Being II** - March 26, 2013
- (Cash Money Records/Young Money Records)
- **Free Weezy Album** - July 4, 2015 (Young Money Records)

HOT BOYS

- **Get It How U Live!!!** - October 28, 1997 (Cash Money Records)
- **Guerilla Warfare** - July 27, 1999 (Cash Money Records)
- **Let 'Em Burn** - March 25, 2003 (Cash Money Records)

OFFICIAL LIL WAYNE MIXTAPES

2002

- **Lil Wayne AND The Sqad SQ1**
- **Lil Wayne AND The Sqad SQ2**
- **Lil Wayne AND The Sqad SQ3**
- **Lil Wayne AND The Sqad SQ4**

2003

- **Lil Wayne AND The Sqad SQ5**
- **Lil Wayne AND The Sqad SQ6**
- **Lil Wayne AND The Sqad: The Remix SQ6**

2004

- **SQ7**
- **Da Drought**
- **Da Drought 2**
- **The Prefix**

2005

- **The Suffix**
- **Dedication: Gangsta Grillz**

2006

- **Lil Weezy Ana Volume 1**
- **Dedication 2: Gangsta Grillz**
- **The Carter Files**
- **The W. Carter Collection**
- **The W. Carter Collection 2**
- **Young Money The Mixtape Vol. 1 (Disc 1)**
- **Young Money The Mixtape Vol. 1 (Disc 2)**
- **Lil Wayne & Julez Santana - Blow: The I Can't Feel My Face Prequel**
- **Lil Wayne, Birdman & DJ Khaled - The Carter 2: Part 2 Like Father, Like Son**

2008

- **Dedication 3: Gangsta Grillz**

2009

- **No Ceilings**

2011

- **Sorry 4 The Wait**

2012

- **Dedication 4: Gangsta Grillz**

2013

- **Dedication 5: Gangsta Grillz**

2015

- **Sorry 4 The Wait 2**
- **No Ceilings 2**

CHAPTER 6
THIS YEAR I GOT A SPACE SHUTTLE PARKED OUT AROUND THE CORNER

Mannie Fresh was born Byron O. Thomas, March 20, 1969.

One half of the game spittin' duo Big Tymers, and the man behind the sound of Cash Money Records, Mannie Fresh sums himself up in four words: Lovely. Wonderful. Exciting. Energy.

Mannie Fresh came up out of the NOLA scene known for his DJ skills and ability to ignite any party with an 808 drum machine and an analogue keyboard. As a teen, he was a member of New York Incorporated and collaborated with MC Gregory D on the seminal New Orleans classic album Throw Down. Relocating to Los Angeles to pursue significant label interest Fresh interned for RCA Records, who released the third Gregory D album, The Real Deal, in 1992. While there, he had a valuable stint learning drum programming under the wings of Chicago House music pioneer, Steve "Silk" Hurley, and played out live dates as tour DJ for Bay Area legends Spice-1 and Too $hort.

Mannie Fresh connected with Cash Money Records CEO, Baby, in 1993, and became the label's de facto in-house Producer. Over time he developed a clear head bobbing signature sound combining Miami Bass and NOLA Bounce with samples, 808 music and raps. His musical vision on the transitional 1996 Cash Money Records release, B.G.'s Chopper City, set the wheels in motion for the whole crew to follow. He jumped on his bandwagon creating a "say what you want type shit" duo with Baby called Big Tymers.

The rest is history with Mannie Fresh bringing his magic to the yard, and it was only a matter of time before nonstop hits began to drop like rain in the Hot Boys, B.G., Juvenile, Turk, and Lil Wayne.

***

Who is Mannie Fresh?

Mannie Fresh:
Lovely. I mean, lovely, wonderful, exciting, energy. That's Mannie Fresh.

Does Mannie Fresh get his due?

Mannie Fresh:
Definitely, man. My due is to see them little kids shine. To see Wayne and them do they thing, that's me.

You're coming up with every track on every album. How do you do that?

Mannie Fresh:
It's just a gift. It's what God gave me to come here and do, so that's what I do. I just put it down like that. It don't take me long or nothing like that.

The sound has changed over the years. There has been much progression.

Mannie Fresh:
You got to change with times. I ain't trying to change too much because right now my shit is the hottest shit right now, ya feel me. So I ain't trying to change too much, but I ain't mad at the dudes that's copying it either 'cause they got to start from somewhere. I just got to be the leader, that's all.

What do you listen?

Mannie Fresh:
Everything, man. James Brown, Bob Marley, Marvin Gaye; almost any and everything. Kiss, Yes, Tears For Fears, you name it I listen to it; Beethoven, Mozart.

Do you listen to any Techno?

Mannie Fresh:
Nah, not really, but if it's jammin', I give it an ear.

Specific tracks like B.G.'s "Thug'n" have that progression.

Mannie Fresh:
It might be something that I might have heard because I'm that type of person. I might be going through the radio with something and hear something new, and if I like the way it is, then I might get an idea from that. Just from listening to some of the tracks a lot of 'em got like Techno feel to 'em. The first thing I was doing a long time ago was Miami Bass, so Miami Bass is kind of close to Techno. The closest thing I think I listen to Techno is probably Kraftwerk.

I hear that with the progressions and the arpeggios.

Mannie Fresh:
Fa sho.

There's some Reggae, especially on the Big Tymers albums.

Mannie Fresh:
I'm digging everything. You give it to me; I'll listen to it.

You're the music man in the family. When was the transition from Bounce to now? How did it come?

Mannie Fresh:
It's just - I just tried to take Bounce to another level. Bounce was just some samples and 808 loops, so I just decided to put some music over it, ya dig? And bring it to another level instead of just using samples, or whatever. I just put some original music over it and used the 808 instead of using a loop. It just eventually got into this. It wasn't nothin' that took forever to do 'cause it was something that I've been doing. I've been doing this since probably like ten years ago. It just kind of caught on.

How did you get your name?

Mannie Fresh:
I'm from the old school. My name is old school. You don't hear nobody calling themselves Fresh or nothing like that. I'm just old school, ya dig? I always been Mannie Fresh. I was the one that came up with new ideas back in the day. I was the one that just was like ... They would be like he comes out with a new scratch or something like that or a new mix, so that's how I got the name Fresh 'cause I used to always come out with new shit.

How did you hook up with Cash Money?

Mannie Fresh:
I've been knowing them from way back in the G, and they just decided to start their record company. At the time I was with a bogus record company, so I was like we gonna hook up and do something, and they was like we gonna go all the way with it. We like, we're gonna go all with it, let's keep it real, ups and downs, and the rest is history. We just talked about it. It wasn't nobody that I met. I've been knowing them. They used to come to parties and stuff I used to be DJing and stuff.

What's a Mannie Fresh set?

Mannie Fresh:
I'm old school. You come around me you might see an old 808 and an old Moog board or something like that. I ain't really into using new instruments and Midi and all that kind of shit. I guess that burn up a lot of Engineers, but that's my thing. That's Mannie Fresh sound, that's Mannie Fresh ways.

Do you produce and engineer?

Mannie Fresh:
Yeah, I do all that.

Do you get any free time?

Mannie Fresh:
Nah, not really, not really. I'm in the studio late tonight. I don't really ... I ain't happy unless I'm in the studio anyway, so it don't matter.

What kind of stuff are you coming up with lately?

Mannie Fresh:
Lately, I've been doing some 80s type stuff like I'm on some ... Plus I'm on some old Disco type stuff, ya feel me? I've been doing Disco shit plus that 80s type sound shit to get away from what everybody is doing, but I'm still incorporating it my way. I listen to a lot of songs and do it my way.

What is the Mannie Fresh way?

Mannie Fresh:
You know, that Bounce feel to it, that dance feel to it, that energy. The shit that gets you up and makes you bob your head. I try to produce tracks from a DJ perspective like the type of music that will get the crowd crunk, that will get it up and running.

What about "Fuck The World" on the 'Lil Wayne album? It's a slow jam in a way and not Bounce.

Mannie Fresh:
That was his thing. That song was more-so made out of him than me, and I just met him like 90-percent of the way in doing the song. It was something that he wanted to get across, so it wasn't nothing that I really could do my way. And it's some real shit that he's spittin', so I felt like I owed him out of respect to do it that way.

How do you balance all the stuff in the Big Tymers?

Mannie Fresh:
Man, the Big Tymers is wild, man. That's just some 'ol say what you want to say type shit. Last time I was talking about helicopters. This year I got a space shuttle parked out around the corner.

Baby:
We ain't rhyming or rapping just talking shit.

How do you come up with the intros to the albums?

Mannie Fresh:
That's natural. It ain't nothin' you think about. We just run it.

Baby:
We don't write shit. We go in there.

Mannie Fresh:
We go in there and run it. What you hear is what you get.

You're just fucking around in the studio, and it's a Big Tymers album?

Mannie Fresh:
Yeah! That's basically what the Big Tymers is. What you hear is what you get.

You did the B.G. albums.

Mannie Fresh:
Yeah.

It was transitional.

Mannie Fresh:
It just grew with time. Back then that's what was going on, that's what was happening. It don't take long for shit to happen and next year they on some other shit. You got to change with it. Back when the first B.G. album came, that's what was going on. It was Mob. Then the next album after that we had some Pimps and shit. Then after that, we had Killers. You got to change with the times.

What are the times now?

Mannie Fresh:
It's all crazy right now. We got Guerillas, man. It's kill or be killed, so you got to go with that.

Anything else to say?

Mannie Fresh:
I want to say I love you, mom.

Cash Money Records issued ***The Mind of Mannie Fresh*** album in December 2004. The single "Real Big" reached #79 on the Billboard charts. Mannie Fresh parted ways with Cash Money Records in 2005 over a perceived royalties dispute. He signed with Def Jam South and maintained a busy studio schedule with a host of artists eager to work with the man who crafted the Cash Money Records sound. Sadly, his sister was murdered in her home in 2007, and Fresh went underground for a few years to handle stressful situations with the loss. He resurfaced in 2009 on Chubby Boy Records with his sophomore solo album, ***Return of the Ballin'***.

Mannie Fresh has spent the past few years as a touring DJ and in the studio with a few artists. He is currently working on a new album, tentatively titled ***The Mind of Mannie Fresh 2***, and on a unique project with Yasiin Bey, formerly known as Mos Def. There is also a rumoured EDM album in the works with Lil Wayne and production team Play-N-Skillz.

MANNIE FRESH ALBUM DISCOGRAPHY

- **The Mind of Mannie Fresh** - December 21, 2004 (Cash Money Records)
- **Return of the Ballin'** - October 27, 2009 (Chubby Boy Records)

BIG TYMERS

- **How You Luv That** - 1997 (Cash Money Records)
- **How You Luv That Vol. 2** - September 22, 1998 (Cash Money Rercords)
- **I Got That Work** - May 16, 2000 (Cash Money Records)
- **Hood Rich** - April 30, 2002 (Cash Money Records)
- **Big Money Heavyweight** - December 9, 2003 (Cash Money Records)

CHAPTER 7
I LOOK AT IT WE GOT TO HUSTLIN'

Baby a.k.a. Birdman was born Bryan Williams, February 15, 1969.

Baby had a rough turn for the first twenty years of his life. His mother died when he was 2. He lived in a boys home and spent some time homeless. As a citizen of the Magnolia Projects, he got by hustling, robbing and selling heroin until arrested for the first time at the age of 16, and then again for drug possession when he went on to serve 22 months incarcerated.

In the early days, he went by B-32, Baby with the 32 Golds. He CO-founded Cash Money Records in 1991 with his brother, Ronald Williams, and together they put in the work, time and energy necessary to make it a success. Among the first artists signed to the label were Kilo-G, Pimp Daddy and U.N.L.V. In 1993, he released his debut solo album, *I Need A Bag of Dope*.

Baby and Cash Money Records in-house Producer, Mannie Fresh, formed like Voltron in 1997 as Big Tymers and recorded their first album featuring the Hot Boys, **How You Luv That**. The dynamic duo instantly became known and loved for their off the cuff shit talking. **How You Luv That Vol. 2** followed in September 1998 as the first new music issued under the landmark pressing and distribution deal with Universal Music Group.

Baby was a man on a mission during the day this interview occurred on the set of the Baller Blockin' film, deep in the heart of the Magnolia Projects. Hard to nail down for a talk, he weaved in and out of our one-on-one conversation and then popped up unannounced to join in with his Big Tymers partner, Mannie Fresh.

***

What do you want people to know about Cash Money?

Baby:
We gonna be the best thing that ever happened to Hip-Hop, for Rap music, period.

Is this the neighbourhood you grew up?

Baby:
Yeah, one of 'em.

What was it like coming up?

Baby:
It was hard. A nigga ain't got nothin' trying to get somethin'. It's just some hard up shit.

How did you put Cash Money together?

Baby:
How I put it together? Me and my brother just came, and Fresh, Geezy, and the Hot Boys and Juve, and we just mashed the shit, put it together and got it where it's at today.

What role do all the jewellery and flossin' play?

Baby:
This was our thing before the deal. We always did wear jewellery and all that shit. We always did wear ice.

Where are you headed with the label? What are you plans?

Baby:
With the Rap game? To be the best ever, the best ever to even fuck with this shit. You know how long it took for a nigga to break OJ Simpson records and

Jim Brown's records? That's how long it gonna take for a nigga to even fuck with me in this game.

You're gonna try to keep it going and going.

Baby:
I'm gonna keep it going. I ain't gonna try; I'm gonna.

How much control do you have over the artists?

Baby:
100% is mandatory. I don't look at it control, that's a business term. I look at it we got to hustlin', we hustlin'. Control ain't the word. You don't control no man. We have Chiefs and Indians out here.

How do you and your brother divide up the duties of running the business?

Baby:
It's an easy divide 'cause it's two of us. I don't find this shit being hard. The only hard thing was for me fucking with this movie 'cause it was a challenge to me. I was doing movies, doing concerts and recording and that shit. That was kind of like a challenge for me.

You're an artist as well with Big Tymers.

Baby:
Yeah.

What's that all about?

Baby:
Game spittin' without a doubt.

***

Big Tymers issued their third album, ***I Got That Work***, in May 2000. It debuted at #3 on the Billboard charts and is known for the singles "Get Your Roll On" and "#1 Stunna".

Big Tymers **Hood Rich** album arrived at the tail end of April 2002. None of the Hot Boys appears on the album, as by this time Lil Wayne was the only one still with the label, but it did not matter as "Still Fly" became their biggest hit, and the album entered the Billboard charts at #1. Baby's sophomore solo album, **Birdman a.k.a. The #1 Stunna**, was issued in late November 2002 and came armed with big money special guests.

Big Tymers **Big Money Heavyweight** came in December 2003 and marked the final release by the duo. Baby then officially changed his name to Birdman.

Birdman's **Fast Money** album released in June 2005. Lil Wayne joined him to record the **Like Father, Like Son** album that was issued on Halloween 2006.

The **#1 Stunna** album arrived on the heels of the trend-setting "Pop Bottles" single in December 2007.

The **Pricele$$** album released in November 2009 is the most recent Birdman solo album. Its fourth and fifth single "Money To Blow" and "4 My Town" feature Lil Wayne and Drake.

Birdman appeared on off the club bangers **Rich Gang** compilation album released in July 2013.

In April 2016, Birdman coined the phrase "put some respect on my name" live on the syndicated The Breakfast Club radio show, hosted by DJ Envy, Angela Yee, and Charlamagne The God. When the video went viral he launched a "Respek" merchandise line to capitalise.

Birdman and Apple announced a deal on August 16, 2016, for an upcoming Birdman and Cash Money Records documentary.

Big Tymers performed a reunion show at the New Orleans House of Blues on October 7, 2016.

The on again, off again relationship between Birdman and Lil Wayne continues to make headlines.

BIRDMAN ALBUM DISCOGRAPHY

- **I Need A Bag of Dope** (1993)
- **Birdman** - November 26, 2002 (Cash Money Records)
- **Fast Money** - July 21, 2005 (Cash Money Recordso
- **Like Father, Like Son with Lil Wayne** - October 31, 2006 (Cash Money Records)
- **5 Star Stunna** - December 11, 2007 (Cash Money Records)
- **Pricele$$** - November 23, 2009 (Cash Money Records)

BIG TYMERS

- **How You Luv That** - 1997 (Cash Money Records)
- **How You Luv That Vol. 2** - September 22, 1998 (Cash Money Records)
- **I Got That Work** - May 16, 2000 (Cash Money Records)
- **Hood Rich** - April 30, 2002 (Cash Money Records)
- **Big Money Heavyweight** - December 9, 2003 (Cash Money Records)

CHAPTER 8

I AIN'T GONNA LET NOBODY ELSE GUIDE OUR DESTINY

"Godfather Slim" was born Ronald Williams, May 23, 1967.

Ronald "Godfather Slim" Williams is the CO-founder of Cash Money Records. He and his brother, Bryan "Birdman" Williams, came up with the Housing Projects of New Orleans hustling before starting the label in 1991 and built its foundation one seed at a time.

Cash Money Records came into the next phase of their growth and development by signing and mentoring B.G. and Lil Wayne as father figures. Eventually pairing them up with Juvenile and Turk to form the Hot Boys. Acting as Father figures and Uncles to their artists who grew up in one parent household, the brothers spent time schooling the Hot Boys by explaining to them morals, discipline and respect on a family trip out of love. Investing their time, energy and money into grooming the hungriest one, B.G., since the age of ten to be the one to lead the crew.

The slow and steady growth plan began to reap the rewards as multiple albums sold in the hundreds of thousands building a groundswell of interest in Cash Money Records. Well educated in the music business, by being prepared to handle the money and fame, and armed with the ability to comprehend and deal with situations. The hard work and dedication paid off large when Universal Music Group bought in, and Cash Money Records changed the face of Hip-Hop.

Not much is known about Ronald "Godfather Slim" Williams. He likes to stay behind the scenes and let his brother, Bryan "Birdman" Williams, bask in the limelight. The number of published interviews with him recorded on the one hand.

***

What is Cash Money?

Godfather Slim:
Man, it's a music thing. We a record company trying to be one of the best ever in this music business. We gonna be the greatest of all time like Muhammad Ali in the music industry.

How will you accomplish that?

Godfather Slim:
By longevity, staying in this game a long time; always putting out good product; always cooperative and be more business with everything we do.

Every decision goes back to you and your brother?

Godfather Slim:
Yeah, in some sense as far as our business moves be we be the Chiefs, but we talk to our people, and we all sit down and go over things, and we all make decisions together whether it's good or bad. Me and my brother get the last word.

What was it like coming up?

Godfather Slim:

A struggle. Well, not a struggle. It's like living in New Orleans is hard off the top 'cause ain't no money here, ain't no jobs. Coming up out here, man. If you don't have - All we got is Football. All we got is sports and entertainment. You got to make a choice. If you work hard ... I see a lot of people go to College and work hard all them years to get a job and still can't get a job, a good paying job. If you got all these tools, like a degree and all that, you ain't promised to get a job. You ain't promised to be - You successful education wise, but as far as survival-wise, it's hard down here. You'll have to move away to get something that suits your needs, as far as your education got you.

You and your brother are very inspirational to all your artists and people.

Godfather Slim:

Yeah, 'cause they look up to us as daddy's and uncles. We teach them like if our father was teaching us; the morals, the discipline, the respect, to respect people and the whole nine, and they respect us for that 'cause they ain't never - Some of them they ain't never had fathers. Some of 'em they ain't never had moms, or their people wasn't there for them. We been there for them other than this music game. We been there for 'em on the love tip, on the family tip 'cause when we was coming up ... My mom died when we was young. All we had was our daddy, and he worked a lot to make sure we had everything, but he never was able to sit down and talk to us as much as he would have liked to, but as a provider, he was providing for us, and we never wanted for nothing else. He did everything that a father could do without a mom.

How did you get into the record game?

Godfather Slim:

We just wanted to find us and find something we like, something we wanted to do. Something that we gonna enjoy and that we'll be happy with, and we all could eat and make people happy and hire some of our friends and hire some people that wouldn't be able to get a job 'cause some of 'em - A lot of our friends are from a lot of penitentiaries. If you got arrested, or your got a conviction, you can't get a job. It's very, very hard for you to get a job, so we employ a lot of people that been in the penitentiary who ain't got the chance. Who where society wouldn't give them that chance to get a job and survive in this world.

How did you start Cash Money Records?

Godfather Slim:
Well - They had this record thing starting to pop in New Orleans, and we was lookin' - It took us a year to find out how to get the business part of it, like the paperwork, the incorporation. We was looking around trying to find out how to get this going and nobody would tell us until we ran across a few people that gave us a little insight on things. Ever since then we've been trying to work this Cash Money thing. It's been working out good for us.

Were there key people who helped put you on?

Godfather Slim:
Our Accountant, she worked and investigated and shared the air, and just her investigation on how to get the incorporation. She got the incorporation situation done for us and the paperwork, and we just ran the label.

How did you hook up with Universal?

Godfather Slim:
Dino Delvaille, who is an A&R at Universal, came down and spoke with us about how things are going with our label. We was doing pretty good, and all in the South and a few other areas and we made some noise. So they came, they said they're keeping an eye out, talked with us, and we did that for about a year. It took us a year because we had a lot of other companies coming around trying to make a deal happen with us too. We was weighing our pros and cons to see which would be the best situation for Cash Money, not only for me and my brother but Cash Money as a whole and our artists.

You own the masters and everything.

Godfather Slim:
Yeah, we own all that. That's what we wanted 'cause we wanted to have control of our situation, and we know one thing. If we was to control our situation, we gonna make it work.

In online newsgroups, a woman named Wendy Day claims she got you signed and received nothing. What's your comment on that?

Godfather Slim:

Man, she didn't get us signed. She didn't sell not one of them records. She ain't get us signed. All she did was out there when we was in New York going to these record labels with us. She ain't done nothing. I don't have nothing against this woman. She caused all this for nothing. We sold these records. We went in and handled our own business. Ain't nobody handles our business for us. We went in and made our own deal. I ain't gonna let nobody else guide my destiny and it ain't right. People gonna say what they want to say, so if that's how she feels do her thing. I wish her the best of luck.

Are people out to get Cash Money and not give you your due? Are people always trying to put you down?

Godfather Slim:

Anything when you're successful they gonna always have they good and they bad. We just put our hands in the hands of God and ask him to weed out the good and keep the bad for us. We know to expect whatever. It won't be no surprise to us whatever happens. We cool with it, whatever.

You seem mellow.

Godfather Slim:

Yeah, I'm mellow. I'm laid back, man. I don't let nothing gets me angry. That's petty. I could put that forward to something else.

What was it like coming up before Cash Money when you were hustling?

Godfather Slim:

It was cool, but it wasn't nothing you can enjoy. It was cool, that's just the way of life the way Blacks come up. You can either do one or the other. You can either go the good route or the bad route, and we choose to leave everything bad to accomplish something good, and by us going the right way making the right decisions, and God got us in the right way, we here and can't nothing stop us.

What kind of business would you recommend for a young entrepreneur on the streets coming up?

Godfather Slim:

This music industry. I would prefer and recommend to anybody to try to do your own, get your own. Establish your own thing. Something that you can control. Something that you can say that's yours and something that you give your ideas and your concepts to 'cause can't nobody express what's in your mind and your heart but you, and have faith in God, and everything you wish and all your dreams will come true.

You're older than these guys. What was the music scene like before?

Godfather Slim:
It was more on the Bounce tip. They got something called Bounce down here. I don't know if you ever heard of it, it was more on a Bounce tip. We used to be on that level doing that.

U.N.L.V. and all that.

Godfather Slim:
Yeah, we done that before, but we had to do that in order to get in and change the game. As sure as days goes by we was changing, and we changed it to this point down here. We couldn't just walk in and say we was gonna rap and the scene was already going on the Bounce thing already. So we had to Bounce our way in and change it to Bounce with lyrics, then we changed it to straight lyrics, so we changed with them. We had to come in and do our thing, man. We put our ingredients to it and made it happen.

Was B.G. the transitional artist?

Godfather Slim:
Yeah.

Why him?

Godfather Slim:

Because he was the most hungriest of all of 'em. He was the one that - The one that we was - While all that was going on with the Bounce thing, we was grooming him; he was ten years old. We was grooming him, and we groomed him to be that one, that one kid, and when we got him there, he just let it loose.

Were you grooming a ten-year-old and placing all your investments in a ten-year-old?

Godfather Slim:

For sure. I believed in him. I done went … I cleaned … We got rid of every artist we had for him. We just kept him 'cause he was no problem. We had artists that was problems, that didn't want to do right, who wanted to be a Rapper but didn't want to be a Superstar. There's a difference from a Rapper and a Superstar. A Rapper go in the studio and lay out his lyrics, and that's that. A Superstar Rapper goes in, do his studio, do his press, do everything comes with the game; promotions, promotional shows; everything came with the game, and he was that person.

He wanted it. He had to move up. He wanted this, like him and Fresh.

He's still maintaining. How have you seen him grow up? Are you proud of his progress?

Godfather Slim:
I'm happy on the music side, yes. Business wise, yes. He got it together. See, these young cats with a lot of money and they handling their situation so good. They're not big headed. They're still the same person with people. They respect people, they respect the elderly and all of it. Everybody can't do that, and that's from our nine years, or eight years, however long we been in this business. That's what made us the people we is 'cause we didn't go from Junior High to the NBA. We went from Junior High, High School, College in this music industry. See everybody ... Some people might have one hit and go straight to the top and then can't handle situations in this business, and we were able to handle the situations because we done went through it all. We know all aspects of this business. We done went through it all. We went through the good times, the bad times. We done went through it all. It's been good for us. I used to be like damn, these people ain't selling more records than us but they getting a deal. But then I thought about it. It wasn't time for us, and now that we at this point here, all them years we waited paid off for us.

What lessons have you learned?

Godfather Slim:
To handle the money and the fame and the attention. That's something that's very important because if you can't handle that your whole ship gonna sink.

What are your comments on No Limit? They stole many of your concepts.

Godfather Slim:
I wish them, people, the best. We don't have nothing against them. We wish them the best. We doing our thing. They doing their thing. That's all I have to say as far as that.

Does it feel good now that you're going up and they're selling less?

Godfather Slim:
We just doing what we got to do. We don't need to worry about them because if we worry about the next person, then you ain't gonna be able to handle your business, so we just handling our business and we ain't even worried about what they do.

What is *Baller Blockin'*?

Godfather Slim:
It's about this Project, New Orleans Project. About some young cats coming up in the hood, the corruption of the Police force. Police want to get in the game of this Project and don't want to - They playin' both - The Police playing both sides of the law, good and bad. It's nice, bro. They gonna love it, trust me. *Baller Blockin'* they will love.

When is it coming?

Godfather Slim:
It's supposed to come for Christmas but we aiming for sometime in the new year.

What else do you have on the horizon?

Godfather Slim:
We got the Big Tymers new album coming out. Juvenile coming out December 14. We got something else coming out in the new year too that we working on, some big major stuff.

How is it different working independent and then now with Universal?

Godfather Slim:
It's more to it that you got to do now. You have more people you have to see and talk to. You have a lot of press. You have a lot of interviews. You got to learn how different operations is setting up records and all that. It's just a little different is all. It's more now.

What else do you want people to know?

Godfather Slim:
We ain't going nowhere. We the unstoppable Cash Money Records. We gonna be here for years. We gonna do what Russell Simmons did in fifteen years in three years.

***

Sometime around 2007, "Godfather Slim" was diagnosed with Marfan Syndrome. A genetic disorder that affects the body's connective tissue in 1 in 5000 men and women of all races and ethnic group. Blessed to be able to afford the testing and surgery, he took it to heart and incorporated a health fair with Cash Money Records annual Thanksgiving turkey giveaway. The market provides valuable screenings for high blood pressure, diabetes, and glucose, eye exams, dental, podiatric services and information booths with healthcare professionals and volunteer nurses onsite.

Cash Money Records allied with Atria Books, an imprint of Simon & Schuster, to distribute Cash Money Content books in late 2010. Beginning in 2011, Cash Money Content has published urban fiction, self-help, and memoirs. In tune with the blueprint of Cash Money Records, the Cash Money Content imprint has quietly sold millions of books they own outright by New York Time bestselling Author, Wahida Clark, the late Iceberg Slim, the ***Murderville*** trilogy by Ashley JaQuavis, and Rev. Al Sharpton. The brand is projected to branch out into the production of television series and films.

In August 2012, "Godfather Slim" paid $7.15 million cash for the most substantial house in Southern Florida. A 34 000 square foot waterfront mansion in the triple-gated Windmill Ranch community located in the city of Weston.

The label introduced Grand Touring Vodka and fronted by Birdman in 2013. Known as GTV, it is six times distilled grain vodka available in regular and infused flavours like watermelon and coconut.

"Godfather Slim" participated in a keynote interview as part of the ***Sync Up Conference,*** produced and presented by the ***New Orleans Jazz & Heritage Foundation***, during the ***New Orleans Jazz Fest*** on April 26, 2014.

REVIEW PLEA

Thank you for reading my book.

I appreciate all of your comments, and I love hearing what you have to say. I need your feedback to make the next book in this series better.

Please leave a helpful review wherever you got this copy letting me know what you thought of this book.

Thanks so much!

WHO IS HARRIS ROSEN?

Father. Son. Brother.

Harris Rosen is the author of **N.W.A: The Aftermath, The Real Eminem: Broke City Trash Rapper**, and other Behind The Music Tales books. For twenty years, he self-published the national lifestyle magazine Peace! He lives in Toronto, Canada, with his son, Louis.

Rosen has interviewed hundreds of composers, artists, actors, and athletes. Including the Notorious B.I.G., Dr Dre, Daft Punk, Eminem, Derek Jeter, Georges St. Pierre, Nirvana, Metallica, Chris Rock, Buju Banton, Beastie Boys, Kiss, Destiny's Child and Aaliyah to list a few.

He has gone to six continents and was in the midst of a whirlwind of multiple musical, cultural revolutions that occurred throughout the 90's and 2000s while compiling a genuine and honest archive of audio, images and video.

behindthemusictales.com
Facebook: behindthemusictales
Instagram: behindthemusictales
Twitter: mrheller1

OTHER BOOKS BY HARRIS ROSEN

BEHINDTHEMUSICTALES.COM

Available Now (print and ePub)

N.W.A: The Aftermath

The Real Eminem: Broke City Trash Rapper

The Real Destiny's Child: The Writing's On The Wall

New York State of Mind 1.0

The Reasonings of Buju Banton, Bounty Killer & Sizzla

The Real 213

The Real MC Eiht: Geah!

The Real Diddy

The Real Daft Punk

BEHINDTHEMUSICTALES.COM

The Real DIDDY
by Harris Rosen

The Real MC EIHT: GEAH!
by Harris Rosen

THE REAL 213
by Harris Rosen

Harris Rosen
The Reasonings of Buju Banton, Bounty Killer & Sizzla

Behind the Music Tales 9.0 — 48 Exclusive Photos
MAGNOLIA — Home of tha Soldiers
Exclusive interviews with the Hot Boys and Cash Money Millionaires
HARRIS ROSEN

BEHIND THE MUSIC TALES 7.0
NEW YORK STATE OF MIND 1.0
EXCLUSIVE 1992-1993 INTERVIEWS WITH TRAGEDY KHADAFI, BRAND NUBIAN, PETE ROCK & C.L. SMOOTH
HARRIS ROSEN

THE REAL DESTINY'S CHILD
The Writing's On The Wall
Behind The Music Tales 6.0
Harris Rosen

BEHIND THE MUSIC TALES OF TRUTH, FICTION & DECEIT 5.0
THE REAL EMINEM
BROKE CITY TRASH RAPPER
HARRIS ROSEN

N.W.A THE AFTERMATH
The Truth In Their Own Words
Exclusive Interviews with Dr. Dre, Ice Cube, Jerry Heller, Yella & Westside Connection
Harris Rosen

www.ingramcontent.com/pod-product-compliance
Lightning Source LLC
Chambersburg PA
CBHW061929290426
44113CB00024B/2854